Approaching Tourism

Approaching Tourism

edited by

Geoffrey Wall

Department of Geography Publication Series

Series Editor   Clare Mitchell
Series Manager   Kate Evans
Cover Design   Monica Lynch
Printing   M & T Insta-Print (K-W) Ltd.

ISBN 978-0-921083-75-7   ISSN 0843-7386

Library and Archives Canada Cataloguing in Publication

Approaching tourism/edited by Geoffrey Wall

(Department of Geography occasional paper, ISSN 0843-7386; #21)
Includes bibliographical references.
ISBN 978-0-921083-75-7

1. Tourism. I. Wall, Geoffrey II. Series.

G155.A1A66 2007   910   C2007-905417-X

Preface and Acknowledgements

Since 1999, the University of Waterloo has run a guest lecture series on tourism research as an enrichment of its tourism offerings. This has brought a variety of established tourism scholars to Waterloo to share their insights on tourism. It has become customary to publish a book as a record of the presentations so that the insights can be shared with others. This publication contains a selection of the lectures that have been presented in recent series. Although the lecture series will continue, this book constitutes the last occasion on which the lectures will be made available in this format. With changing technology, virtually all presentations have associated powerpoint presentations and these have been posted, with the permission of the authors, on related websites.

The lecture series and this book would not have come into existence in the absence of the commitment and patience of a number of people.

First, I wish to thank the speakers who gave freely of their time and knowledge to travel to Waterloo to make their presentations. Without exception, their stimulating lectures raised awareness of the complexity and variety of tourism issues, and the diversity of ways through which they can be explored.

From the outset, the Dean of the Faculty of Environmental Studies, initially Dr. Geoff McBoyle and, more recently, Dr. Deep Saini, have been enthusiastic supporters of tourism research and education, as has Dr. Paul Parker, Chair, Department of Geography.

Dr. Clare Mitchell, a colleague in the Department of Geography, and editor of the Department of Geography Publication Series, read the entire manuscript.

Special thanks are due to Kate Evans who skillfully turned a collection of manuscripts into a book and forged ahead with the manuscript when inputs from the editor of this volume were lacking. This publication constitutes the last publication in this series. Kate has given great service to the Geography Publication Series over the years. The editor of this volume has benefited greatly from her diligence and patience in preparation of volumes based on the tourism lecture series as well as in other ways. This preface, therefore, presents the opportunity to thank Kate not only for her work on this and previous volumes, but to wish her well in her future endeavours.

Dr. Geoffrey Wall
Professor of Geography

Table of Contents

Figures

Tables

Measuring Tourism

Stephen Smith

INTRODUCTION

Policy, planning, marketing, and forecasting in tourism depend on having accurate numbers. It is also a common experience to read claims that tourism is the world's largest industry or to hear media stories about the impact of events such as SARS or the War in Iraq on the number of visitors to a country and their levels of spending. From where do these numbers come? How good are they? Why do some estimates of the size of the tourism industry – in terms of contributions to the economy or jobs created - vary so much? This chapter explores these issues in the context of Canadian tourism statistics. The chapter begins with an overview of some of the challenges of measuring tourism and then turns to solutions developed in Canada to deal with these problems. Finally, some statistics about the magnitude of Canadian tourism are presented.

HISTORICAL CHALLENGES IN TOURISM STATISTICS

Tourism in Canada is a large and fragmented sector of the economy. It consists of more than 156,000 enterprises in a variety of industries that produce a broad range of services (the nature of tourism industries will be discussed below). These businesses are found in virtually every community. They range in size from small, one-person ("sole proprietorship") operations such as someone with an ice cream stand at a beach, to large, multi-national operations such as Fairmont Hotels and Resorts. However, tourism enterprises overwhelmingly are small. For example, the World Travel and Tourism Council (WTTC, 2001a and 2001b) estimates that 95 percent of the world's tourism firms are SMEs – small and medium enterprises (which the WTTC defines as establishments with fewer than 10 employees). And perhaps because tourism enterprises are predominantly small enterprises, the tourism sector generally has little tradition of using research or supporting either the collection or application of data on the sector. The lack of demand by industry for credible statistics has been compounded by historical problems that further harmed the credibility and utility of tourism statistics. These problems have included: inconsistent definitions, confusion about the nature of tourism, inadequate data sources, double-counting, and the lack of a connection of tourism statistics (especially revenues and expenditures) with the System of National Accounts.

Inconsistent Definitions

Tourism statistics have often lacked credibility in the eyes of decision makers because different definitions of tourism have been used, each resulting in different estimates of the size of tourism. For example, some definitions include business travel as part of tourism, others exclude it. Some require an overnight stay, others do not. Some define tourism in terms of trips over a certain distance, others define it in terms of crossing political boundaries. Some include capital investments in airports, roads and sewer systems as part of tourism's contribution to the economy; others exclude these. Some include retail shops selling primarily to visitors as part of the tourism industry, others exclude them.

Confusion about the Nature of Tourism

These differences reflect the fact that many researchers and policy analysts have been (and sometimes still are) confused about the nature of tourism. Some see tourism as a set of businesses and organizations serving the needs of visitors. Others include such businesses but expand the sector to include businesses that serve the needs of tourism businesses, as well. Others consider tourism to be a set of activities engaged in by persons temporarily away from their home environment. Jafari (1992) abstracts the various perspectives on tourism as belonging to four paradigms or "platforms". The first (in Jafari's terminology) is the "advocacy" platform, which focuses on tourism's contributions to job creation and economic development. The "cautionary platform" takes an opposing view by pointing out the costs of tourism. The "adaptancy" platform recognizes both benefits and costs of tourism and argues that proper planning and management can ameliorate problems while still achieving benefits of tourism. Finally, the "scientific" platform focuses on the objective understanding of tourism as a phenomenon. Given the diversity of fundamental perspectives on the nature of tourism - intrinsically good, intrinsically bad, a management and planning problem, or a subject for scientific research – confusion about the nature of tourism is not surprising.

Inadequate Data Sources

One result of these problems is that data sets from different sources cannot be meaningfully compared because they are founded on different assumptions and definitions. Moreover, given the size and diversity of tourism enterprises and the fact that visitors are found in so many different destinations and that visitors often resist completing surveys – tourism data sets often are too small or too laden with non-response and other sources of bias to produce reliable data. National-scale surveys can be expensive to implement and will be undertaken only if there is a strong mandate by industry or political leaders who see the need for reliable data for informed decision-making. This, historically, has not been the case in Canada.

Potential for Double-Counting

The potential for double counting also contributes to the lack of credibility in some tourism data. Double counting is not intentional but can occur when a researcher utilizes data from two or more different sources. For example, a hotel with a restaurant and bar may report restaurant and bar sales together in one document and separately in another document. If a researcher is not careful about the purpose, coverage and conventions used in secondary data sources, food and beverage sales (in this example) could be counted twice. As another example, US visitors to Atlantic Canada typically visit two or three Atlantic Provinces. If someone simply counts the number of Americans visiting each province and then adds them, the same visitor will be counted two or more times.

Lack of Connection with the SNA, NAICS, CPC

The definition and measurement of industrial inputs and outputs in a nation's economy is governed by a macro-economic accounting system know as the System of National Accounts (SNA). The SNA is an internationally accepted framework for measuring the size and activity of national economies. In an over-simplified way, the SNA can be thought of as a series of large spreadsheets. One of these is the "Make Matrix", which consists of a large number of rows representing various commodities, and the columns representing industries. Each cell contains the dollar value of the output of each industry by commodity. Generally each industry will be characterized by a dominant commodity – airlines, for example, are characterized by the production of passenger air transportation services. However, each industry may also produce other commodities. Airlines, for example, produce some food and beverage services through the sale of alcoholic beverages onboard their flights. Another matrix, the "Use Matrix", provides information on the total value of each commodity used (as an input) in the industry's production process.

The industries included within the SNA are identified in a classification system known as the North American Industrial Classification System (NAICS); the commodities produced by industry are categorized according to the Central Product Classification system (CPC) (United Nations Statistics Division, 1990). In Canada, the SNA recognizes 216 industries and 623 commodities.

While many tourism services, such as air transportation and hotel rooms, are recognized as distinct products produced by distinct industries (passenger airline transportation and accommodation industries, respectively), tourism *per se* does not appear in either the NAICS or CPC. This has made measurement of tourism as a sector in the economy a particular challenge, especially when one wishes to be able to compare, on a credible basis, the magnitude of tourism with conventional industries.

Beyond the omission of tourism from the SNA and associated classification systems, another problem for tourism statistics is that any establishment can be classified into only one category. The decision about which category is based on the business's primary source of income. If the establishment mentioned in the preceding paragraph derived most of its revenues from the letting of its rooms on a nightly basis, it would be classified in the NAICS category of 9111, "hotels, motels and tourist courts". This classification would apply whether the hotel offered only rooms, or a restaurant, convention services, a fitness club, and a gift shop along with the rooms. This can be a particular problem in the case of government-owned and operated attractions such as museums, parks and historic sites. While each of these types of operation is a type of tourism enterprise, the fact that many are operated by government agencies means that they are classified under the dominant activity of government agencies – public administration. Their contribution to tourism in terms of revenues is simply missed because it is assigned to "public administration".

A NEW AGE OF TOURISM STATISTICS

Tourism statisticians and economists have long recognized the challenges described above and have been working since the 1930s to solve these problems. A brief history of these efforts can be found in Smith (2000). For the purposes of this chapter, it is sufficient to note that the so-called Ottawa Conference on the Statistics of International Travel and Tourism, sponsored by the World Tourism Organization in 1991, represented the dawn of a new era in tourism measurement. Delegates at that conference achieved an international and official consensus on the definition of tourism and related concepts, and advanced an innovative analytical framework for allowing the measurement of tourism's contribution to national economies to be calculated in a way that conforms to the conventions of the SNA - the Tourism Satellite Account.

Fundamental to the new developments that support the measurement of tourism in ways that permit greater accuracy, consistency and comparability than ever before is the definition of tourism. This definition was developed under the aegis of the World Tourism Organization and endorsed by more than 160 nations (WTO, 1994):

> *Tourism* is the set of activities of persons travelling to and staying in places outside their usual environment for not more than one year and for any purpose other than the pursuit of remuneration from within the place visited.

There are several key aspects of this definition:

1. It is a demand-based definition. It conceptualizes tourism as something people do, not as something businesses produce.
2. Tourism involves more than just pleasure travel. It includes study tours, personal travel, business travel (as long as the purpose of the trip is not to earn money from the place being visited), pilgrimages, travel to seek health care, and so on.
3. Expenditures to be measured are generally limited to those made by the traveller or on behalf of the traveller (such as by a travel agent or the traveller's employer) in the context of a specific trip. Investments in infrastructure or equipment by businesses or government are not counted as tourism expenditures.
4. Tourism involves travel away from home – outside the usual environment. The operational definition of usual

environment is not specified, but it means that tourism is not something one does in one's home town.

5. Length of stay can be less than one day (not overnight) and up to a year. Any trip longer than a year is implicitly considered to be a change in residence.

Several other definitions were developed at the Ottawa Conference that are important in guiding the development of a tourism statistical infrastructure (WTO, 1994). These are the following:

> A *visitor* is a person engaged in a tourism trip.

> A *same-day visitor* is a person who takes a tourism trip and returns home the same day.

> A *tourist* is a visitor who takes a tourism trip that keeps him away one night or more.

> A *tourism commodity* is any good or service for which a significant portion of its demand comes from visitors; in other words, it is a good or service that would be produced in substantially reduced quantities (or not produced at all) in the absence of tourism.

> A *tourism industry* is any industry whose characteristic or dominant commodity is a tourism commodity. The notion of an industry is a hierarchical concept – one can speak of a hotel industry, of a roofed accommodation industry (hotels, motels, bed-and-breakfasts, resorts), a general accommodation industry (that would include campgrounds), or an even more general hospitality (accommodation and food services) industry. Each subsequent industry in this list is more general than the preceding industry.

Tourism is conceptualized as existing in six forms, three of which are elemental, and three of which are combinations of the elemental forms:

Domestic tourism is tourism involving persons travelling only within the country of their residence.

Inbound tourism is tourism involving persons arriving from another nation to spend time in the country of destination.

Outbound tourism is tourism involving persons leaving the country of their residence to visit another country.

National tourism is the combination of domestic and outbound tourism. In other words, it refers to all tourism activity by residents of a nation regardless of where that tourism occurs.

Internal tourism is the combination of domestic and inbound tourism. In other words, it refers to all tourism activity in a nation regardless of whether visitors are residents or not.

International tourism is the combination of inbound and outbound tourism. In other words, it is all tourism that involves crossing an international border.

One other term should also be defined, although this definition is not part of the set of tourism definitions established by the WTO.

An industry is a group of businesses producing essentially the same commodity using essentially the same technology in a volume that represents a substantial value of output. In Canada, in 2003, the threshold for production of a group of businesses to be considered a distinct industry is $200 million in gross revenues.

Given these concepts, one can examine why the SNA does not consider tourism to be a distinct industry. The range of industries that produce tourism commodities is quite diverse. It includes transportation (whose core products involve moving people around), accommodation (whose core products involve keeping people in one place), and recreation and entertainment services (whose core product involves entertaining people). These industries also utilize widely diverse technologies. Transportation usually involves a vehicle with some form of engine or motor guided by a pilot/driver/captain/engineer, which may or may not be the traveller himself. Accommodation services typically utilize fixed buildings, some sort of check-in system and reservation service, the provision of beds and plumbing facilities, housekeeping services, and so on. There is no plausible way in which these diverse industries can be aggregated to represent a "tourism industry". Thus, there is no tourism industry recognized in the SNA, although there are tourism industries.

Although tourism commodities are characterized by having a substantial part of their total demand generated by visitors, tourism commodities are also consumed by people not engaged in tourism. For example, local residents patronize restaurants. Persons changing their residence (migration is not considered to be tourism) utilize airlines and hotels. Conversely, visitors also consume commodities that are not tourism commodities: clothing, sun screen lotion, telecommunication services, dry cleaners, crafts, groceries, books and beer and wine.

Moreover, tourism industries may produce non-tourism commodities in limited amounts. Hotels sell laundry services and telecommunication services, and many have retail shops selling clothing and notions. Some non-tourism industries produce tourism commodities: department stores may operate restaurants or travel agencies. These observations can be generalized as four core dilemmas in measuring tourism as an economic activity.

1. Visitors and non-visitors consume tourism commodities.

2. Visitors and non-visitors consume non-tourism commodities.

3. Tourism industries produce tourism and non-tourism commodities.

4. Non-tourism industries produce tourism and non-tourism commodities.

The challenge in developing a framework to measure the economic magnitude of tourism is to devise a method for extracting from the System of National Accounts those portions of production and consumption that can be meaningfully linked to tourism, using the WTO definition of tourism. Such a method has been developed – the Tourism Satellite Account (TSA) (Lapierre and Hayes, 1994). The term "satellite" simply means that it is an extension of the SNA. The TSA is a complex, multi-layered, quantitative information system that adds a tourism dimension to the SNA. It defines a synthetic industry, an amalgam of portions of conventional industries that can be interpreted statistically to be the tourism industry. Because the TSA is an extension of the SNA, the results of the TSA can be compared to the results of other analyses of the SNA. For example, one can compare the value of tourism production with the value of the production of the agricultural industry. It is important to remember though, that all the production and consumption values in the TSA have been extracted from other industries – so one cannot simply add tourism's output to that of other industries to make some sort of aggregate estimate. This would be double counting. Another important feature of the TSA, as an extension of the

System of National Accounts, is that production and consumption must balance. The total supply of a commodity must be equal to the total consumption of that product (including inventories, exports, and consumption by whatever source of demand – consumers, businesses, governments).

TSAs require substantial amounts of high quality data. These data describe both the supply-side and the demand-side of tourism. Table 1.1 summarizes some of the key sources of data used in the Canadian TSA.

Table 1.1: TSA Data Sources

Supply-Side Data Source	Demand-Side Data Sources

Input-Output Tables from SNA
Business income tax returns
Business Censuses and survey, such as
    Airlines
    Restaurants, caterers, taverns
    Travel agencies and tour operators
    Attractions
    Accommodations
	Canadian Travel Survey
	International Travel Surveys
	    Canadians returning home
	    US visitors entering Canada
	    Offshore visitors entering Canada
	Family Expenditure Survey

The input-output tables are the heart of the SNA, providing information on the value of each commodity category consumed by each industry as well as the value of each commodity produced by each industry. A sample of business income tax returns is examined by Statistics Canada researchers, on a confidential basis as permitted by Federal legislation, to obtain supplemental information on the financial inputs and outputs of different types of businesses as well as expenditures for labour (payroll and payroll taxes). Business censuses and surveys provide additional, detailed information on the cost and revenue structures of various types of tourism businesses as well as insights into the range of commodities they produce.

The Canadian Travel Survey is an ongoing monthly survey of Canadian households in Canada (over the course of a year) to collect information on trips taken, trip characteristics, trip spending, and other travel-related behaviour. The International Travel Surveys are also an ongoing survey that collects similar information for Canadians returning from international trips, US visitors coming into Canada (they represent about 80 per cent of total inbound tourism and many are same-day visitors) and offshore visitors entering Canada.

The Family Expenditure Survey, done every few years, is a significant study of household expenditures on a wide variety of commodities. These include the consumption of tourism commodities by both persons engaged in tourism, as well as people not involved in tourism (such as local residents dining at a local hotel restaurant).

Utilizing these concepts, definitions and tools allows Canadian researchers to develop a tourism statistical infrastructure. This infrastructure consists of not only the core surveys and the TSA, but also the National Tourism Indicators, a set of over 300 data time series describing various aspects of tourism demand, supply and employment. The following statistical summaries are drawn from these sources.

EXAMPLES OF TOURISM STATISTICS

Before presenting some statistics describing the magnitude of tourism in Canada, two more terms need to be defined. *Tourism demand* refers to the level of expenditures in a given year on various commodities. *Supply* refers to the total value of a commodity that is produced. Both demand and supply are measured in terms of dollar values. Even for commodities such as hotel and passenger air transportation, not all the supply of a commodity is consumed by a visitor. The portion of demand for tourism commodities that is attributable to spending by visitors is shown in Table 1.2. Accommodation generally has the highest percentage of demand from tourism – over 90 per cent – compared to other major tourism commodities. Restaurants receive about one-quarter of their demand from visitors. These percentages reflect national averages over the course of a year. Commodities sold by individual business-es will vary dramatically from these averages, depending on the time of year and the location of the business.

Table 1.2: Per Cent of Tourism Demand in Total Demand by Selected Commodity

Commodity	%
Passenger air transport	92.1
All passenger transport	42.4
Hotels	91.4
All accommodation	93.8
Meals from accommodation	51.8
Meals from restaurants	25.9
Recreation and entertainment	27.7
Travel agencies and tour operators	97.8
Groceries	2.8
Alcohol from retail stores	1.6

Source: Lapierre and Hayes, 1994

Table 1.3 presents the absolute volume of demand and supply for aggregated tourism commodities. The largest Canadian tourism industry, in terms of revenues, is transportation, followed by "other tourism" (which includes convention fees, travel agents and tour operators, and recreation and entertainment) and food services, both over $8 billion. Total spending on tourism commodities was over $44 billion in 2001. However, as noted, visitors also buy other com-modities such as clothing and groceries. Total spending by visitors on tourism and non-tourism commodities was over $51 billion in 2001. These basic patterns held true in 2002, as well.

The pattern of tourism supply, though, is somewhat different. Transportation is still the largest industry, reflecting in part the demand for air passenger services because of the geographic size of

Canada and its dispersed population. Food services is the second largest commodity, at over $42 billion in 2001. As can be seen in Table 1.2, the greatest disparity between supply and demand (reflecting relatively lower tourism demand as part of total demand) is in food services.

Table 1.3: Tourism Demand and Supply: 2000 – 2002 (Billion $)

Commodity	2001		2002	
	Demand	**Supply**	**Demand**	**Supply**
Transportation	19,714	52,573	19,865	54,225
Accommodation	7,848	8,753	7,604	8,442
Food Service	8,246	42,184	8,515	43,671
Other Tourism	8,320	21,294	8,339	21,699
Total Tourism Commodities	44,128	124,804	44,324	128,037
Total Tourism Expenditures	51,663	n/a	51,795	n/a

Source: National Tourism Indicators, Statistics Canada, 2002 and 2003.

Tourism in Canada is characterized by highly seasonal variations in demand, reflecting both annual climatic cycles as well as the social tradition of elementary and secondary schools being closed during the summer. Table 1.4 summarizes seasonal variations in demand for selected commodities. Q3 – July, August, and September – is the dominant tourism season. The annual tourism cycle can be seen as a strong summer peak followed by two quarters of off-season, with a slow thawing during Q2.

Table 1.4: Seasonal Variations in Tourism Demand: 2002 (Billion $)

Commodity	Q1	Q2	Q3	Q4
Transport	4,139	4,995	6,385	4,345
Accommodation	1,375	2,097	2,587	1,545
Food and Beverage Service	1,477	2,050	3,327	1,661
Other Tourism Commodities	1,580	2,034	2,999	1,718
Total Tourism Commodities	8,580	11,175	15,299	9,270
Total Tourism Demand	9,764	12,927	18,115	19,989

Table 1.5 summarizes employment by industry (it should be noted that the rows in Table 1.5 are industries, whereas the rows in Table 1.2, 1.3, and 1.4 are commodities). Food and beverage service is the leading source of employment, although the accommodation industry is a close second. Total employment is over 460,000 jobs, with over another 110,000 jobs generated in non-tourism industries.

Table 1.5: Employment Generated by Tourism: 2001 – 2002 (thousands of jobs)

Industry	2001	2002
Transportation	83.5	78.7
Accommodation	135.2	136.5
Food and Beverage Services	137.6	140.2
Other Tourism Industries	106.6	108.9
Total Tourism Industries	462.9	464.2
Total Tourism-Supported	577.0	579.7

Source: National Tourism Indicators, Statistics Canada. 2002 and 2003.

With the TSA, it is possible to estimate statistically the magnitude of tourism's contribution to the economy (as percent of GDP) in terms consistent with conventional industries. It should be repeated, though, that the contribution of tourism to the national economy is also contained within conventional industries, so these percentages cannot be meaningfully added to generate any sort of total. To do so would be to double count. Table 1.6 summarizes the business sector share of GDP generated by tourism and selected industries.

The various tourism industries contribute differentially to total GDP. Table 1.7 summarizes the relative share of each tourism industry to total tourism GDP.

Table 1.6: Business Sector Share of GDP by Industry: 2001

Industry	% of GDP
Manufacturing	23.4
Finance, insurance, real estate	19.8
Community, business, and personal services	15.4
Wholesale trade	7.0
Retail trade	6.7
Construction	6.3
Mining, quarrying, and oil drilling	4.6
Other utility industries	4.1
Communications	3.8
Transportation and storage	3.6
TOURISM	3.2
Agriculture and related services industries	1.6
Logging and forestry	0.7
Fishing and trapping	0.2

Source: Special Tabulation, Statistics Canada, 2001.

Table 1.7: Tourism GDP by Industry: 2001

Industry	% of Tourism GDP
Air transportation	16
Other transportation	14
Accommodation	21
Food and beverage services	15
Other tourism industries	8
Other (non-tourism) industries	23

Source: Special Tabulation, Statistics Canada, 2001.

Tourism is a significant contributor to government revenues. Through business and personal income taxes, property taxes; GST/PST/HST on tourism purchases; excise taxes on fuel and alcohol; payroll taxes; licensing fees such as for cars, boats, fishing, and hunting; and admission fees to public facilities, about 31¢ of every visitor dollar ends up as government revenues. Table 1.8 summarizes the relative contributions by level of government.

Table 1.8: Tourism-Generated Government Revenues

Level	% of Tourism Dollar
Federal	16.8
Provincial	12.1
Municipal/Regional	2.1

Source: Special Tabulation, Statistics Canada, 2001.

SUMMARY

Industry leaders, government officials and academics have finally recognized the accurate measurement of tourism as a form of economic activity as essential for effective policy formation, planning and marketing decisions. However, simply recognizing the need is far from sufficient. The development of a tourism statistical infrastructure requires substantial sustained funding, political will and a vision for what is needed. International consensus on key concepts and definitions, as well as the development of new analytical tools to solve some of the technical and conceptual complexities of tourism as a form of economic activity also are required. Significant progress has been achieved since 1990 and much of this has been led by Canadian tourism statisticians and economists.

Canada developed and published the world's first Tourism Satellite Account and played a significant role in having the TSA designated by the United National Statistical Commission as the standard methodology that nations should adopt when measuring tourism in their economies. However, TSAs require a substantial database including statistics on tourism demand (domestically as well as internationally) and supply. Once these data are in place and sustained by an ongoing, well-funded program of data collection, it is possible to provide – for the first time – objective, reliable and comparable national-level tourism statistics.

REFERENCES

Jafari, J. (1992) "The scientification of tourism," in S.A. El-Wahab abd and N. El-Roby (eds.), *Scientific Tourism*, Cairo: Egyptian Society of Scientific Experts on Tourism, 43-75.

Lapierre, J. and Hayes, D. (1994) "The tourism satellite account," *National Income and Expenditure Accounts, Quarterly Estimates, Second Quarter*, 1994: xxxiii - lvii.

Smith, S.L.J. (2000) "New developments in measuring tourism as an area of economic activity," in W. C. Gartner and D. W. Lime (eds.), *Trends in Recreation, Leisure, and Tourism*, New York: CABI Publishing, 225-234.

United Nations Statistics Division (1990) *International Standard Industrial Classification of all Economic Activities (ISIC), Revision 3*, New York: United Nations.

World Tourism Organization (1994) *Recommendations on Tourism Statistics*, Madrid: WTO.

World Travel and Tourism Council (2001a) *Building Human Capital*, London: WTTC.

World Travel and Tourism Council (2001b) *Competitiveness Monitor*, London: WTTC.

2

Pilgrimage and Tourism in the Holy Land: The Christian Case Study

Noga Collins-Kreiner

INTRODUCTION

The chapter deals with the relationship between pilgrimage and tourism in modern Israel. It focuses on the case of Christian pilgrimage to the Holy Land and discusses the theoretical and practical implications of this connection.

The relationship between tourism and religion has focused primarily on the question of the similarity and difference between the tourist and the pilgrim (Cohen, 1992; 1998; Smith, 1992; Vukoni'c, 1996). This research is a continuity of this ambivalent subject and offers a point of departure for other studies in Christianity and religious tourism as well as other contexts and religions.

Even though religious tourism as a niche in the international tourism market has grown in recent years, not much has been published on this topic from a tourism viewpoint. For example, only one book has been written specifically looking at tourism and religion (Vukoni'c, 1996). This is surprising, as it is impossible to understand the development of leisure and, therefore, tourism, without studying religion and understanding the pilgrimage phenomena in ancient times.

The chapter begins with a discussion of definitions, theories and facts related to the pilgrimage - tourism relationship. Then, a Christian Pilgrimage case study is presented, including the methods used and the findings. The aim of this case study is to broaden our knowledge of the Christian pilgrimage phenomena and to add to previous studies. A theoretical discussion follows, and some practical implications of the phenomena of Christian pilgrimage in the Holy Land are presented. A short summary concludes the chapter.

PILGRIMAGE - TOURISM RELATIONSHIP
Pilgrimage
Pilgrimage is well known and is found in each of the main religions in the world: Islam, Judaism, Buddhism, Hinduism and Christianity. Pilgrimage is defined as "a journey resulting from religious causes, externally to a holy site, and internally for spiritual purposes and internal understanding" (Barber, 1993:1) or as "a journey undertaken by a person in search of holiness, truth, and the sacred" (Vukoni'c, 1996).

In the current literature, there is a high level of uniformity between the pilgrims' beliefs and sites among the different religions. Thus, it is possible to view pilgrimage as an independent phenomenon that cuts across religions and cultures and which has uniform patterns and concepts.

Pilgrimage is an interdisciplinary field and, in recent years, pilgrimage has been studied by researchers from many disciplines: historians, theologians, sociologists, psychologists, anthropologists and geographers. Thus, Sopher (1967) synthesized the state of research in the geography of religions, Turner (1969, 1973) and Turner and Turner (1978), investigated behavioral aspects of pilgrimage and Nolan and Nolan (1989), studied the location and characteristics of pilgrimage to Christian Holy sites in Europe. Eade and Sallnow (1991) advocated an integrated view of pilgrimage. Carmichael (1994) focused on 'Holy Geography and Topography'. Cohen (1992, 1998), Smith (1989, 1992) and other researchers have studied the complex ties between tourism and pilgrimage.

A survey of relevant literature reveals a meager body of sociological theories about pilgrimages. An exception is Eliade's (1969,

1985) concept of the "center of the world" through which passes the 'axis mundi' (the central pivot of the world), providing a plausible context for a theory of pilgrimage. From the perspective of Eliade's concept, a pilgrimage is a religiously-motivated journey to the center of the world itself, or to one of its homologous representations. For the individual pilgrim, that center may also be remote, in the sense that he or she lives at a distance from it, but this remoteness is, in Eliade's interpretation, only locational-geographical and has no theoretical significance.

In contrast, in the Turners' concept of the location of the pilgrimage centers, this remoteness gains theoretical significance. Turner and Turner (1969) introduced several fundamental ideas into the study of pilgrimage, channeling the study of these phenomena into entirely new paths. The Turners' basic idea was that pilgrimage might be analyzed in homologous terms, proposed in their concept of the 'ritual process'. The Turners argued that pilgrimages typically involve a stage of liminality, resembling that in which novices find themselves in the transitory stage between two established social statuses.

Another one of the Turners' fundamental ideas was that pilgrimage centers are typically located 'out there'. This peripherality is both geographical-locational and cultural; the sites are marginal to population centers, and indeed to the socio-political centers of society. These peripheral centers are often located beyond a stretch of wilderness or some other uninhabited territory, in the 'chaos' surrounding the ordered 'cosmicized' social world. Nevertheless, because it is a focus, the pilgrimage center is a paradoxical conceptualization that emerges as a "center out there" (Turner, 1973: 211-214; Turner and Turner, 1978: 241).

Cohen (1992) portrays a typology of pilgrimage centers that can be construed in terms of the relative emphasis on each of these tendencies. Specifically, he proposes distinguishing two polar types of pilgrimage centers: the formal and the popular. Formal centers are those in which the serious and sublime religious activities are primarily emphasized; the rituals at such centers are highly formalized and decorous, and conducted in accordance with orthodox precepts. Though folklorist elements are not absent, they play a secondary role, and are even sometimes suppressed by the authorities. The pilgrims' principal motive for journeying to such centers is to perform a fundamental religious obligation, to gain religious merit, to make a vow or to improve their chances of salvation. The principal pilgrimage centers of a religion, often constituting the apex of a pilgrimage system, come closest to this type of center; the Ka'aba of Mecca, the Church of the Nativity in Bethlehem, St. Peters in Rome, are important contemporary examples of this type.

The Pilgrimage - Tourism Connection
The relationships between tourists and pilgrims have been acknowledged for several decades by medieval scholars and by tourism historians (Smith, 1992) and have been a subject of further research in recent years (Vukoni'c, 1996).

In its current usage, the term 'pilgrimage' connotes a religious journey, but its Latin derivation from peregrinus allows broader interpretations, including foreigner, wanderer, exile, and traveler, as well as newcomer and stranger. The term 'tourist' also has Latin origins, from tornus - an individual who makes a circuitous journey, usually for pleasure, and returns to the starting point. The contemporary use of the terms, identifying the 'pilgrim' as a religious traveler and the 'tourist' as a vacationer, is a culturally constructed polarity that veils the motives of the travelers (Smith, 1992).

Tourism has been defined as an activity dependent on three operative elements: discretionary income, leisure time and social sanctions permissive of travel. Pilgrimage also requires these elements (Smith, 1989). The Turners have claimed that a tourist is half a pilgrim, if a pilgrim is half a tourist (Turner and Turner, 1978).

Others such as Graburn (1989) link tourism to the pleasure periphery and describe tourism as a 'sacred journey' in which the individual escapes from the secular everyday world to the land of play.

Smith (1992) identifies tourism and pilgrimage as opposite end points on a continuum of travel (Figure 2.1). The polarities on the pilgrimage-tourism axis are labeled as sacred vs. secular and between the extremities lie almost infinite possible sacred-secular combinations, with the central area (c) now generally termed 'religious tourism'. These positions reflect the multiple and changing motivations of the traveler whose interests and activities may switch from tourism to pilgrimage and vice versa, even without the individual being aware of the change. Jackowski and Smith (1992) use the term 'knowledge-based tourism' as synonymous with religious tourism. Most researchers identify 'Religious Tourism' with the individual's quest for shrines and locales where, in lieu of piety, the visitors seek to experience the sense of identity with sites of historical and cultural meaning (Nolan and Nolan, 1989).

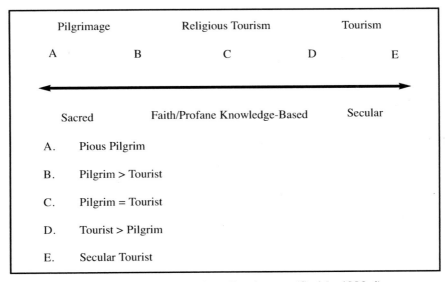

Figure 2.1: The Pilgrimage - Tourism Continuum (Smith, 1992:4)

Contemporary research deals with the complicated relationship between pilgrimage and tourism, including the economic, political, social, psychological, emotional, and other aspects. Representative of this connection are Eade's (1992) article, which both describes the interaction between pilgrims and tourists at Lourdes and Rinschede (1992) and develops a typology of tourist uses of pilgrimage sites, and the Nolans' work on Christian sites in Europe (1989, 1992). Specific papers on Christian pilgrims to the Holy Land have been written by Bowman (1991); Fleischer and Nitzav (1995); Collins-Kreiner and Kliot (1997); Fleischer (2000) and Kliot and Collins-Kreiner (2002).

The nature of 'tourist experience' has received a lot of attention from tourism research (Turner and Turner, 1969, 1978; MacCannell, 1973; Cohen, 1979, 1992). MacCannell (1973) was the first to claim that it is a quest for the authentic, and that it presents the pilgrimage of modern man: the tourist is perceived as a pilgrim in the current modern secular world.

Cohen (1979) proposed a continuum as a discriminating distinction between five types of tourist experience. It is based on the place and significance of tourist experience in the total world-view of tourists: their relationship to a perceived 'center' and the location of that center in relation to the society in which the tourist lives. One can not describe 'the tourist' as a "general type" (Cohen, 1979: 180). Therefore, there are several tourist experiences that will help in the understanding of the phenomena of pilgrimage. Five main modes are defined, presenting the spectrum between the experience of the tourist as a traveler in pursuit of 'mere' pleasure, and that of the modern pilgrim, in quest of meaning at someone else's center. He classifies them as the "Recreational mode", the "Diversionary mode", the "Experiential mode", the "Experimental mode" and the "Existential mode" (Cohen, 1979: 183). Cohen claims that tourists traveling in the "existential mode" are analogous to pilgrims. Both are fully committed to an elective spiritual center, external to the mainstream of their native society and culture because they feel that the only meaningful "real" life is at the center.

Cohen's (1992) research on tourist and pilgrim activities at sites in Thailand claims that pilgrimage and tourism differ in terms of the direction of the journey undertaken. The 'pilgrim' and the 'pilgrim-tourist' peregrinate toward their socio-cultural center, while the 'traveler' and the 'traveler-tourist' move in the opposite direction. This distinction applies particularly in regard to journeys to formal pilgrimage centers. However, journeys to popular pilgrimage centers, which are typically 'centers out there', will often be marked by a mixture of features characteristic of both pilgrimage and tourism.

Many attempts are underway, indicating that the difference between old-fashioned pilgrimage and tourism is narrowing. Numerous points of similarity are emerging, and the word 'pilgrimage' itself is widely used in broad and secular contexts, such as for visits to war graves or the graves and residences of celebrities: for example, Elvis Presley's mansion and tomb in Memphis (Reader and Walter, 1993).

Religious Tourism To Israel

Israel contains many sites sacred to the three monotheistic religions. Religious travel nowadays to Israel is made by Christians, Jews, Moslems, Bahai, Druze, Mormon and others. There are many holy sites concentrated in a relatively small piece of land: 290 miles (470 km) in length and 85 miles (135 km) in width at its widest point.

It is important to note that each religious authority administers its corresponding site and shrine, and the law ensures freedom of access and worship. The main holy sites in Israel classified by religious affiliation are:

- Judaism: The Kotel, the Western ("Wailing") Wall, the last remnant of the retaining wall of the Second Temple, and the Temple Mount, in Jerusalem. Rachel's Tomb, the Tomb of the Patriarchs in the Cave of Machpela in Hebron; the tombs of Maimonides (Rambam) in Tiberias, the Tomb of Rabbi Shimon Bar Yohai in Meron and many others.

- Islam: Haram al-Sharif building complex on the Temple Mount, including the Dome of the Rock and Al-Aqsa mosque, in Jerusalem. The Tomb of the Patriarchs in Hebron, the El-Jazzar mosque, in Akko.

- Christianity: Via Dolorosa, the Room of the Last Supper, the Church of the Holy Sepulchre and other sites of Jesus' Passion and Crucifixion in Jerusalem; The Church of the Nativity in Bethlehem, the Church of the Annunciation in Nazareth, the Mount of Beatitudes, Tabgha and Capernaum and the Sea of Galilee (Lake Kinneret).

- Druze: Nebi Shuieb (tomb of Jethro, father-in-law of Moses), near the Horns of Hittin in Galilee, Nebi Sabalan, Nebi Yaafori.

- Bahai (independent world religion founded in Persia, mid-19th century): Baha'i world center, the Shrine of the Bab in Haifa, the Shrine of Baha'u'llah, prophet-founder of the Baha'i faith, near Acre.

The annual number of tourists coming to Israel was around two million in 1995-2000 (Israel, Ministry of Tourism, 2001). The estimations are that 25 per cent of all the tourists are Christian pilgrims (Fleschir, 1995; 2000). Another 40 per cent of all the tourists are Christian who come with different and varied motivations, but usually pay a visit to the Christian holy sites. Jewish tourists are about 25 per cent of all the tourists and they come for multiple reasons-usually including religious motives. About five per cent are Moslems (Mansfeld and Ron, 2000). Religious tourism is one of the biggest tourism market segments today in Israel and it is estimated that religious tourism will grow in the future, all over the world and in Israel, depending on the political situation.

The 'Christian Experience' in the Holy Land: A Case Study

The purpose of this research is:

- to describe, characterize and analyze the characteristics of Christian pilgrims to holy sites in the Holy Land at the present time;

- to identify the market segment of Christian pilgrims to the Holy Land; and

- to help to redesign the 'Christian Product' of the Holy Land.

The Holy Land has always been the main destination of Christian pilgrims from all over the world. Pilgrimages to the Holy Land and its sites, especially to Jerusalem, Bethlehem, Galilee and Nazareth, are known to have taken place as far back as the 2nd century (Colby, 1983). Roman Catholics and Protestants constitute the majority of the incoming pilgrims to the Holy Land. The number of pilgrims increases every year and reached a peak at the millennium - the 2000th anniversary of the birth of Jesus. As an industry, religious tourism, has a unique management and information system. For this reasons it is important to be aware of the needs of modern-day pilgrims to Israel.

Research Aims and Methodology

The method of research used was based on two sets of question-naires in different languages, which the pilgrims were asked to complete. The first set was done between January 1994 - December 1994 and included 100 questionnaires and the second set included 454 'before and after' questionnaires completed between September 2000 - March 2002. Since the results of the second research are in progress, only the findings from the first set of questionnaires are presented in this chapter.

Other methods used were: examination of itineraries of Catholic and Protestants Pilgrimage groups, interviews with tour agencies and tour leaders and 'active observation'.

The questionnaires focused on the expression of the beliefs, feelings, motivations, behaviour and experiences of the pilgrims who were identified as such by their leaders and tour organizers. The research took place at different holy sites in Israel. For Christians all over the world, the Holy Land is synonymous with the life of Jesus. Jerusalem, Bethlehem, Nazareth, Capernaum, Tabgha and the Sea of Galilee, where Christianity started, are today sym-bols of Christian holiness (Figure 2.2).

The pilgrims were asked about personal details and character-istics such as age, country of origin, length of stay in Israel, socio-economic status, number of visits to the Holy Land and denomina-tional affiliation. They were also asked how they would describe themselves, what their motivations for the pilgrimage were, and about the tourist context of the pilgrimage. The pilgrims were also asked about the effect of the political situation in Israel and the visit's implications.

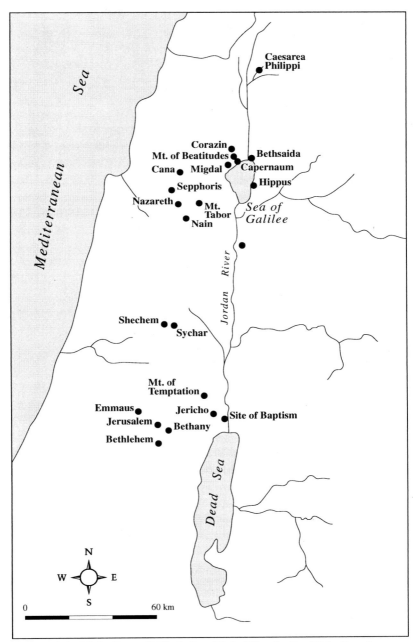

Figure 2.2: Main Sacred Christian Holy Sites in the Holy Land.

Findings

The pilgrims' age distribution curve differs from that of the ordinary tourist visiting Israel, as can be seen in Figure 2.3. While 42 per cent of all incoming tourists to Israel are aged between 41-50 years of age, the proportion of those less than 41 years of age is larger than those over 50 years. However, only 20 per cent of all pilgrims are under 50 years, 50 per cent range between the ages of 51- 60 years, 30 per cent are more than 50 years and 10 per cent of the last group are older than 71 years. The mean age is 55 years - a fact that points to the higher age of the pilgrims.

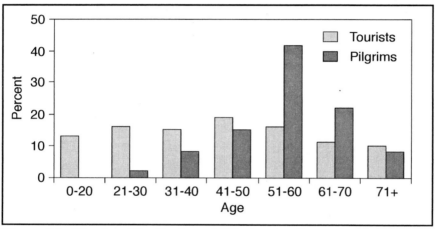

Figure 2.3: The Age Distribution of Pilgrims in Comparison to the Age Distribution of Tourists to Israel.

From the pilgrims sampled, 62 per cent belong to the Roman Catholic Church whose members around the world comprise more than half of all Christians; and 38 per cent belong to Protestant Churches. As regards their socio-economic status, most of the pilgrims described it as medium-low (46 per cent) or as medium-high (43 per cent). Only eight per cent described their status as high and three per cent described it as low - a fact indicating that although most of the pilgrims are not in the high income group, they do come to visit the Holy Land, despite the high cost of travel.

The parameters of age, socio-economic status and denominational affiliation were found to be the most important for the purpose of the analysis. Parameters such as gender and nationality were found to have less influence on the link between pilgrimage and tourism. Accordingly, these parameters were omitted.

The Self-Perception of the Pilgrims

The pilgrims were requested to describe themselves as pilgrims, tourists, or both, or whether they would choose a different description (Figure 2.4). Their choice was based on their own understanding of these descriptions and there was no attempt to influence the interviewees. This self-description is very important because although their leaders classified them as pilgrims, in order to understand the connection and continuum between pilgrims and tourists, it is important to clarify whether the pilgrims' own perception fits this description. The interviewees had the choice of locating themselves on a continuum of pilgrim-tourist.

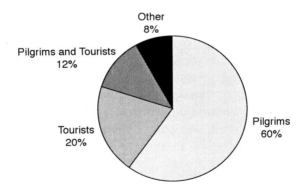

Figure 2.4: The Distribution Diagram of All the Christian Pilgrims' Self Perception.

The findings showed that 60 per cent of the people questioned described themselves as pilgrims, while only 20 per cent classified themselves as tourists, and 12 per cent perceived themselves as both pilgrims and tourists. About eight per cent preferred to describe themselves differently, and not by any of the conventional descriptions. Examples of these unique definitions are: "A Christian with a concern for Israel"; "A tourist following the Bible"; "A friend of Israel"; "A student of the Bible"; and "A walker after the Bible" (*sic*).

Differences in self-perception were found according to the church affiliation (Figures 2.5, 2.6). Most of the Roman Catholics (77 per cent) described themselves as pilgrims, whereas only 35 per cent of the Protestants viewed themselves as such. A third of the Protestants (32 per cent) saw themselves as tourists whereas only 11 per cent of the Roman Catholics viewed themselves as such. No link was found between the pilgrims' ages and their self-image.

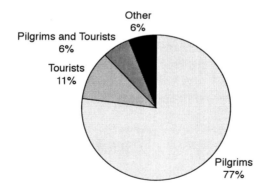

Figure 2.5: The Distribution Diagram of the Roman Catholic Pilgrims' Self-Perception.

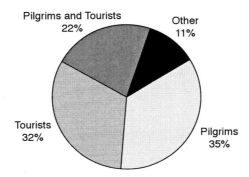

Figure 2.6: The Distribution Diagram of the Protestant Pilgrims' Self-Perception.

An interesting connection was found between the self-image and the ranking of socio-economic status. Those who defined themselves as "pilgrims" tended to describe themselves as belonging to a low socio-economic group, while those who described themselves as "tourists" tended to depict themselves as belonging to a high socio-economic group. All this seems to indicate that the better the economic status of the pilgrim, at least in his own perception, the more likely he was to describe himself as "a tourist". Conversely, the lower his economic status, as perceived by him, the more likely he was to define himself as "a pilgrim".

The question arises: does this trend reflect reality or only a self-image of the socio-economic status and a pattern of behavior on the pilgrim-tourist axis? Do the "high status" people act like tourists and the "low status" people act like pilgrims? Does it follow that, if you come from a certain high socio-economic group, you will be classified as a tourist and if you do not belong to this group you will be described as a pilgrim? If this is only a perceived connection, then all of the self-descriptions are based only on the interviewees' own self-perception and not on their real life socio-economic status. All the respondents' descriptions are based on the continuum between a religious pilgrim and a secular tourist. The variety of

responses presents the problematic differentiation between the pilgrim-tourist and tourist-pilgrim definitions.

The Motivations for Pilgrimage

For those who perceived themselves either as tourists or as pilgrims,
their main reasons for visiting the Holy Land were specified as
being personal and religious. Most of the motives cited may be
regarded as "pull motives" of the Holy Land and not as "push
motives" from the travelers' place of origin. The major reasons
mentioned were "to get to know the Bible" (66 per cent) and "to
improve the religious faith" (59 per cent). Other reasons stated
were, for example: "to strengthen my belief"; "to walk where Jesus
walked"; "to be in the places which are sacred to my religion"; "to
understand from where Christianity started"; "I did not come for a
vacation, but to know Jesus' land"; "to make the Bible live" and "to
understand things from my heart". Most of the reasons pointed to
personal motives, strongly tied to religion, and to a wish to understand one's spiritual inner being.

An interesting discovery prevailing among many of the people
questioned was the conflict between their self-portrayal as tourists
(not pilgrims) and the purely religious reasons, which they mentioned for their visit. It demonstrates how the location on the tourist-
pilgrim axis relates to both self-declaration and motivations for the
visit. Only a few interviewees declared their "pull motives" for visiting the Holy Land to be non-religious reasons, such as a wish to
see something different, and these respondents were the ones who
described themselves as tourists from the very beginning.

For a fifth (21 per cent) of all visitors, the visit to the Holy Land
was associated with a vow they had made to God or to themselves
before they came, which is clearly a religious motive. They
described mental or practical wishes, such as: "to pray with local
Christians"; "to be open to God and to say thank you to him"; "to
pray to understand the Bible"; "to receive God's love"; "to take a

break"; "to get closer to God"; "to pray for the Jews", and "to be a man of belief". It is clear that most of the vows are not connected to a certain act or site, and are more in the way of concepts than practical plans or ideas. They are an integral part of the personal and religious reasons mentioned before for visiting the Holy Land: a wish to get closer to religion, to belief, to get closer to God, and to search for something previously lacking.

A similarity was found between the pilgrims from both denominations in the process preceding their visit to the Holy Land. Most of those questioned (62 per cent) declared that they had wished to visit Israel for more than ten years, a few even "since childhood", "for many years" or for "more than 30 years", etc. This consistency testifies to the special nature of the visit to the Holy Land and to the fact that its motivations are religious, spiritual and from strong belief.

The Tourist Context of the Pilgrimage

An attempt was made to examine the tourist context of the pilgrimage to the Holy Land by asking the visitors direct questions about this aspect of their trip. Forty-one per cent of the pilgrims were not at all interested in these questions and preferred to ignore them. Some of them stated that they ignored these questions because this was not their motivation for visiting the Holy Land, and one of the pilgrims even wrote, "The Holy Sites should not be dealt with a tourist point of view". In general, the Protestants had more comments about the tourist aspect of their visit (71 per cent) than the Roman Catholics, 52 per cent of whom commented.

A few pilgrimage sites were specifically mentioned by the visitors as venues which they did not enjoy. These could be divided into three main categories:

1. Sites where new churches and buildings were built on the
    ruins of ancient ones, such as Capernaum. These additions
    were found to spoil the site's religious and holy authentic-
    ity (Figure 2.7).

Figure 2.7: The New Church of Capernaum.

2. Sites that were found to be noisy, touristy, dirty and commercialized, such as Nazareth, Tiberias and Kafr Kana. An interesting point raised by the respondents is that these sites are becoming like ordinary cities and tourists sites throughout the world and are losing their special spiritual quality (Figure 2.8).

Figure 2.8: The 'Everyday' City of Nazareth.

3.   Sites which are not authentic, such as the baptismal loca-
     tion on the Jordan River - the Yardenit site. Some pilgrims
     mentioned that the fact it is not the "genuine" site spoilt
     their enjoyment when visiting it.

On the whole, pilgrims do tend to complain about the touristic
and commercialised nature of sites and of their lack of authenticity.
Interesting differences in this respect were found between
Protestants and Roman Catholics, regardless of their country of origin. While the Roman Catholics complained about the crowded
sites and the noise and dirt in places such as Nazareth, Tiberias and
Kafr Kana, the Protestants complained about the lack of authentic
feeling at sites such as at the Baptismal site of the Yardenit; the construction of new churches at the ancient sites, for example,
Capernaum; and the fact that today places (such as Nazareth), do
not look as they did in Jesus' time.

Most of the visitors (72 per cent) expressed an interest in visiting sites other than The Holy Christian ones. They were especially
interested in visiting holy places of other religions, and archaeological excavations, and less interested in visiting nature reserves or
other types of tourist attractions (Figure 2.9).

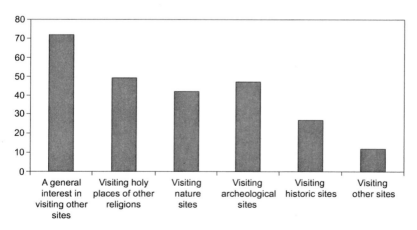

**Figure 2.9: Expressed Interest in Visiting Sites Other Than The Holy
Christian Sites.**

The Protestants, who showed more of a leaning toward tourism, were found to be more interested than the Roman Catholics in visiting sites other than religious ones. While the Roman Catholics wanted to visit holy places of other religions, the Protestants were mostly interested in visiting historic and archaeological sites, such as Acre and Megiddo, and even mentioned cultural and leisure sites (Figure 2.10). The Roman Catholics, then, are closer to the purely religious edge of the religious-secular axis, while the Protestants seem to be closer to the tourist edge of that axis.

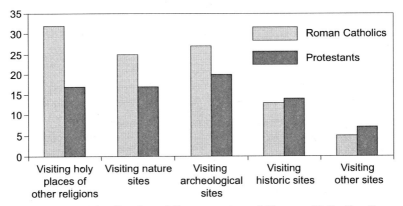

Figure 2.10: The Distribution of Protestants and Roman Catholics By Their Interest in Visiting Sites Other Than The Holy Christian Sites.

Only half of the pilgrims (51 per cent) were interested in activities other than religious ones. Forty-three per cent of the pilgrims were interested in cultural pursuits and 35 per cent of them in shopping. Only 42 per cent of the Roman Catholics were interested in non-religious activities during their visit, especially in shopping - a common activity, which this group feels, does not contradict the religious atmosphere. This is in contrast to most of the Protestants (66 per cent) who preferred to participate in activities such as cultural shows or lectures in addition to the religious visits.

The Effect of the Political Situation and the Implications of the Visit

Most of the pilgrims (81 per cent) agreed to answer the questions on the political situation in Israel and on their personal security during their visit. Only a third (26 per cent) mentioned previous reservations about personal safety. In contrast, 71 per cent felt absolutely confident during their visit. The process can be identified as fear before arriving in Israel, changing to a feeling of confidence, thanks to their leader, the local population, and especially to their belief in God. The result is particularly surprising, seeing that their stay in Israel lasted a few days only. It was enough, however, to give them a good, secure feeling. There was a difference between Roman Catholics and Protestants, however. Whereas 50 per cent of the Roman Catholics felt insecure before arriving, only 20 per cent of the Protestants felt that way. As mentioned above, this situation changed on reaching the Holy Land.

Only a minority answered that they were affected by the Jewish-Arab conflict (16 per cent) or by the peace process in the area (31 per cent). These factors were expressed in general contexts such as: "I pray for peace in the region". This finding is surprising if compared to the official publications of the Ministry of Tourism, which state that the political situation does affect tourists' decision to come to Israel. A possible explanation of this paradox is that those who did come to Israel were not affected by the political situation. The possibly non-religious tourists who did not arrive were those who were discouraged by security considerations.

A clear-cut consensus was found concerning the effect of their visit to the Holy Land: almost all the pilgrims (80 per cent) will definitely recommend that their friends come on a pilgrimage to the Holy Land. Many of the pilgrims (70 per cent) felt that their visit would reinforce their religious feelings and would also deepen their religious knowledge, with no relation to their age or church affiliation. Both Roman Catholics and Protestants were satisfied with their visit (67 per cent), felt their expectations had been fulfilled (77 per cent), and were interested in another visit to the Holy Land (67 per cent).

DISCUSSION: THE TOURISM-PILGRIMAGE AXIS

One of the conclusions relates to the existence of a continuum upon which the features characterizing the pilgrims can be ranked. This continuum is composed of secularism versus sacredness and tourism versus pilgrimage. On the one side, near the sacred and pilgrimage end, we have "pure" pilgrims who are interested only in holiness and worship, and on the other side we have "pure" tourists who are interested mainly in the modern tourist aspects of their visit. Each visitor may be ranked on this scale according to his motivations and interests. A "pure" pilgrim is located near the sacred edge, while a tourist is located near the tourism edge. A visitor who reveals the self-image of a tourist but expresses religious motivations, feelings and wishes is located near the tourism - sacred side. On the other hand, a visitor who defines himself as a pilgrim but expresses a wish to visit non-religious sites and whose motives are not entirely religious, is located near the pilgrimage-secular side.

The differences that were noted among the visitors' attitudes to the tourist content were found to be dependent mainly on their church affiliations and not on their age, country of origin, socio-economic status, self-perception, etc. The differences depended on the concepts and beliefs of each Christian denomination. Every pilgrim's world perception and his/her self-image on the pilgrim-tourist continuum was ranked according to his beliefs.

We could locate the different Christian denomination and pilgrims on the scale of tourism and pilgrimage according to their attitude towards tourism. Most of the respondents preferred to ignore the touristic aspect of their visit. They did not think it necessary or relevant. About a quarter of all pilgrims saw themselves as "pure" pilgrims and were not interested in any activity other than the religious one. The rest were interested in varying degrees, in visiting different sites and participating in other activities. Most of the visitors questioned preferred to portray themselves as "pilgrims" nearer the religious edge of the religious-secular continuum, and not as "pilgrim-tourists" nearer the tourist edge.

The major pilgrimage motivation for Roman Catholics is to gain inspiration and strengthen belief. These pilgrims come to the Holy Land in order to get closer to their belief and strengthen their faith in a way that will enable them to continue their life back home with new energy and a feeling of purpose. The significance of their visit is derived from the awareness of Jesus' inspiring "presence" at the sites. At the same time, the pilgrims are certain that this awareness will make them more conscious of the spiritual aspect of life (Bowman, 1991). It is, in fact, crucial for them to visit the site itself and to understand the meaning of what happened there. The Roman Catholics perceive themselves as pure pilgrims who concentrate on the religious aspects and disregard the touristic ones. This fact will stand out by the Roman Catholics' location closer to the religious edge of the continuum scale of pilgrimage and tourism as presented here. Practically, their attitude is illustrated by their lack of interest in taking part in secular activities; in ignoring the touristic aspect of pilgrimage; in reversing development of tourist facilities and not mixing holiness and secularism during the pilgrimage itself.

The Protestants believe in direct contact between the believer and the Bible. That is why, for these visitors, building a church at a site seems to detract from its authentic atmosphere (Bowman, 1991). They want to "feel Jesus", directly and not by means of intermediaries. They prefer simple places, such as the Sea of Galilee and its surroundings, to religious and artificial sites such as churches and buildings built at the different sites, because they believe in the spiritual aspect of the pilgrimage and not in the physical aspect. In addition, they are interested in different non-religious activities, in visiting sites that combine religion and history, and in getting to know Israel and its residents. This is why they are classified as being closer to the tourist edge of the pilgrim-tourist continuum and to the prototype of the "Religious Tourist" more than to the pure profile of a "Pilgrim". The Protestants do not ignore the tourist aspect of pilgrimage, such as different tourist facilities at the sites, the mixing of cultural and sporting activities with religious activities, or secular visits to secular and non-Christian sites. Therefore, they are classified as religious tourists and are ranked in the middle of the axis.

The location of each pilgrim on the scale is personal and subjective and between the extremities lie almost infinite sacred-secular combinations. According to Smith (1992), these positions try to reflect the multiple and changing motivations of the traveller whose interests and activities may switch from tourist to pilgrim and vice versa, without the individual even being aware of the change. The researcher can only try to locate the traveller on the scale theoretically, according to parameters such as Christian denomination, self-perception, socio-economic status, motivations, feelings, behaviour and the importance given to different activities.

The conclusions give ground to the theories presented at the beginning of the article on the main themes. The research findings about the common search for meaning, which exists with pilgrims and with pilgrim-tourists, helps to confirm Cohen's (1979) typology of several tourist modes, and to reassert the complex connection between tourism and pilgrimage. It was found in this research that the visitors of the Holy Land are analogous to tourists in the "Existential Mode" (Cohen, 1979). The research finding of a scale existence also reinforce the theory of a new emerging connection between tourism and pilgrimage presented earlier (Smith, 1992). It is becoming more difficult to differentiate between pilgrims and tourists. The pilgrims' motives are to undergo an experience that will add meaning to their life. They leave their periphery to find a center that will offer them a stronger belief and a 'New World'.

This research also confirms Cohen's findings from 1992, claiming that pilgrimage and tourism differ in terms of the direction of the journey undertaken. The "pilgrim" and the "pilgrim-tourist" peregrinate toward their socio-cultural centre, while the traveler and the "traveler-tourist" move in the opposite direction. The participants were described as pilgrims and "pilgrim-tourists" because they traveled from their periphery towards their center. Non-Christian visitors or non-religious Christian visitors to the same places would be "tourists". The difference is not merely one of classification, rather, the attitudes and demeanor of the different kinds of visitors will be wholly different, and so probably will be the meaning and consequences of the respective visits for themselves and for their destination.

The findings also suggest that the phenomenon of 'pilgrimage tourism' is part of 'Heritage Tourism'. This entails travel to sites for a variety of reasons, including nostalgia for the past, the development of identity in terms of place and self, discovering family roots and improving awareness and understanding of historical events and places, which necessarily involve components of history, patriotism and nationalism (Olsen and Timothy, 2002) and strong elements of religious tradition and beliefs. 'Heritage tourism', as a blend of religious, cultural and leisure motives, is emerging today and spiritual feelings are mixed with leisure and recreational.

PRACTICAL IMPLICATIONS
Most of the visitors define themselves as pilgrims and not tourists and their motives are only religious. An emphasis should be placed on Christian religious marketing. For example, the authenticity of the site is more important than accommodation, tour guides, food and transportation.

The religious motive also guarantees a wish to visit The Holy Land even during a problematic political period. This presents a better opportunity for Israel to recover from its current slump in tourism than do other tourism segments such as eco-tourism, leisure tourism etc. Therefore, most of Israel's' efforts should be geared toward religious tourism.

The economic reason was given as the main reason for delay in visiting the Holy Land. Therefore, an effort must be made to reduce the cost of the packages to Israel (for example-accommodation, transportation, guiding etc.) In addition, packages should be planned differently for religious groups from different affiliations.

The pilgrims make their journey as communities with their leaders. It is of great importance to invite priests to visit the Holy Land because they, in turn, will encourage their followers to do the same, as part of their religious commitment.

Tourism scholars have barely focused on tourism policy and management of sacred sites as it pertains to religious sites (Shackley, 2001). It should be noted that religious sites differ from other sites due to their functional and symbolic nature. The simplest example would be that most of the religious sites do not charge money for entering. The challenge facing the religious tourism sector is therefore to strike a balance between tourism and religious heritage management.

SUMMARY

This chapter has focused mainly on the relationship between pilgrimage and tourism. One of the main conclusions is the existence of a scale upon which the features characterizing present-day pilgrims can be rated. Questionnaires as a research method permit an in-depth look into pilgrimage and its ties to tourism. The case study, which is discussed, reveals that pilgrimage constitutes an independent area of research and may be viewed comprehensively. The tourism-pilgrimage phenomenon requires additional research through which the connection between pilgrimage and tourism may be compared, vis-a-vis the perception of those participating in the phenomenon in different religions and countries. A comparative study between pilgrims and tourists is recommended for further research, leading to a better understanding of the multiple connections between the two kinds of movement in today's modern world. It is suggested that the term of 'Pilgrimage Tourism' would fit the characteristics of the phenomena described in this chapter.

REFERENCES

Barber, R. (1993) *Pilgrimages*, London: The Boydell Press.

Bowman, G. (1991) "Christian ideology and the image of a Holy Land: the place of Jerusalem in the various Christianities", in M. Sallnow and J. Eade (eds.), *Contesting the Sacred: The Anthropology of Christian Pilgrimage*, London: Routledge, 98-121.

Carmichael, D.L. and Hubert, J. *et al.* (1994) *Sacred Sites, Sacred Places*, London: Routledge.

Cohen, E. (1979) "A phenomenology of tourist experiences", *Sociology*, 13(2): 179-201.

_____ (1992) "Pilgrimage centers: concentric and excentric", *Annals of Tourism Research*, 19(1): 33-50.

_____ (1998) "Tourism and religion: a comparative perspective", *Pacific Tourism Review*, 2: 1-10.

Colby, P.S. (1983) "Christianity and Christian Holy Sites in the Galilee", in A. Soffer, A Shmueli, and N. Kliot (eds.), *The Lands of Galilee*, Haifa: Haifa University and Tel Aviv Ministry of Defence, 521-528 (Hebrew).

Collins-Kreiner N. and Kliot, N. (2000) "Pilgrimage tourism in the Holy Land: the behavioural characteristics of Christian pilgrims", *GeoJournal*, 50(1): 55-67.

Kliot N. and Collins-Kreiner, N. (forthcoming) "Wait for us - we're not ready yet. Holy land preparations for the new millennium - the year 2000" *Current Issues in Tourism*.

Eade, J. (1992) "Pilgrimage and tourism at Lourdes, France", *Annals of Tourism Research*, 19(1): 18-32.

Eade, J. and Sallnow, M.J. (1991) *Contesting the Sacred: The Anthropology of Christian Pilgrimage*, London: Routledge.

Eliade M. (1969) *The Quest: History and Meaning in Religion*, Chicago: University of Chicago Press.

_____ (1985) *Symbolism, the Sacred, & the Arts*, New York: The Crossroad Publishing Company.

Fleischer, A. (2000) "The tourist behind the pilgrim in the Holy Land", *Hospitality Management*, 19: 311-326.

Fleischer, A. and Nitzav, Y. (1995) *Christian Pilgrims - The Tourism Potential for Peripheral Regions in Israel*, Rehovot: Development Study Center (Hebrew).

Graburn N.H. (1989) "Tourism: the sacred journey", in V.L. Smith (ed.), *Hosts and Guests - The Anthropology of Tourism*, Philadelphia: University of Pennsylvania Press.

Israel, Central Bureau of Statistics (1994) *Tourism and Hotel Services Statistics Quarterly*, Jerusalem: Ministry of Tourism, 21(3) (Hebrew).

Jackowski, A. and Smith, V. (1992) "Polish pilgrim-tourists", *Annals of Tourism Research*, 19(1): 92-106.

MacCannell D. (1973) "Staged authenticity: arrangements of social space in tourist settings", *American Journal of Sociology*, 79(3): 589-603.

Mansfeld, Y., Ron, A. and Gev, D. (2000) *Moslem Tourism to Israel*, Haifa: University of Haifa, Center for Tourism, Pilgrimage and Recreation Research.

Nolan, M.L. and Nolan, S. (1989) *Christian Pilgrimage in Modern Western Europe*, Chapel Hill: The University of North Carolina Press.

_____ (1992) "Religious sites as tourism attractions in Europe", *Annals of Tourism Research*, 19(1): 68-78.

Olsen D.H. and Timothy, D.J. (2002) "Contested religious heritage: differing view of Mormon history", *Tourism Recreation Research*, 27(2): 7-16.

Reader, I. and Walter, T. (1993) *Pilgrimage in Popular Culture*, London: The Macmillan Press.

Rinschede, G. (1992) "Forms of religious tourism", *Annals of Tourism Research*, 19(1): 51-67.

Shackley, M. (2001) *Managing Sacred Sites*, London and New York: Continuum.

Smith, V.L. (1989) *Hosts and Guests - The Anthropology of Tourism*, Pennsylvania: University of Pennsylvania Press.

_____ (1992) "Introduction: the quest in guest", *Annals of Tourism Research*, 19(1): 1-17.

Sopher D.E. (1967) *Geography of Religions*, London: Prentice Hall.

Turner, V.W. (1973) "The center out there: Pilgrim's goal", *History of Religions*, 12(3): 191-230.

Turner, V.W. and Turner E. (1969) *The Ritual Process*, London: Routledge.

_____ (1978) *Image and Pilgrimage in Christian Culture*, New York: Colombia University Press.

Vukoni'c, B. (1996) *Tourism and Religion*, London: Elsevier Science Ltd.

3

Approaching Tourism Through Climate

Geoff McBoyle

INTRODUCTION

Climate along with cost and scenery are the major players in the decision-making of many tourists (Anderssen and Colberg, 1973). Yet for over 30 years researchers have been commenting on the need for more collaboration between climatologists and tourism researchers so that we may understand the role climate plays in tourism and measure its impact. As Hobbs in 1980 stated, "Little is known in quantitative terms about the effects of weather conditions on recreation and tourism."

Thirteen years later Smith (1993:398) commented strongly about the lack of collaboration – "meteorologists and leisure specialists rarely communicate with each other" and in 1997 Perry reiterated the call for collaboration when he concluded:

> New research initiatives are urgently needed into the effects of climate, observed and perceived, on tourism which will require more collaboration between applied climatologists and tourism specialists, p.247.

Part of the difficulty is that climate conditions are not the only factor influencing tourism decisions so that it is not easy to tease out the direct links between climate and tourist choices and tourism decision-making (Smith, 1993; Perry, 2000).

Most of the research undertaken on climate and tourism has been published in the climatological and geographical literature by climatologists (Paul, 1972; Perry, 1972, 1997, 2001; Hobbs, 1980;

de Freitas, 1990, 2001; Abegg *et al.*, 1997). In the tourism literature, this topic has not figured prominently (Agnew and Palutikof, 2001) although in the last decade articles on the impact of climate change on tourism have appeared by tourism experts (Wall, 1992; Lohmann and Kaim, 1999; Lohmann, 2001), climatologists (Giles and Perry, 1998) and economists (Harrison *et al.*, 1999). However, when tourism experts and climatologists collaborate, worthwhile results are produced such as the research on climate change and winter recreation activities by Wall, McBoyle and Scott, and others (McBoyle *et al.*, 1986; McBoyle and Wall, 1987; Wall and McBoyle, 1992; and Scott *et al.*, 2001 and 2002).

CONCEPTUAL FRAMEWORKS

Conceptual frameworks for understanding the links between climate and tourism have been presented by de Freitas (1990:91, 2001) and Lohmann and Kaim (1999). de Freitas' framework is based heavily on the heat balance of the body (the thermal conditions) although it includes physical aspects ("specific meteorological elements, such as rain or high wind, which directly or indirectly affect participation satisfaction other than in a thermal sense") and aesthetic components such as visibility, sunshine or cloud which Limb and Spellman (2001:7) say may lend "light, colour, character, movement and atmosphere to scenery". These three aspects are correlated to a nine point weather rating based on the American Society of Heating, Refrigerating and Air Conditioning Engineers (ASHRAE) (Winslow *et al.*, 1938). This atmospheric condition rating may be used in recreation-weather forecasting, recreation-climate land assessment and facility planning.

On the other hand the framework from Lohmann *et al.* (1998) published in Lohmann and Kaim (1999) indicates clearly that weather is one of the many factors affecting the attractiveness of an area and depending on demand and communication, this attractiveness may result in some action that could develop an area for tourism or could draw an individual there as a tourist.

Accepting that participation in tourism/recreation is conditioned by a range of social, economic and other environmental factors, a conceptual framework is presented (Figure 3.1) which takes as its focus how individuals, such as tourism facility developers, tourism operators, tourism marketers and tourists use and/or could use climate to assist their decision-making. Because each of these stakeholders has a different time horizon for their decision-making, tourism, as Smith stated in 1993, has to be viewed as either weather sensitive (short term) or climate sensitive (long term) (Table 3.1).

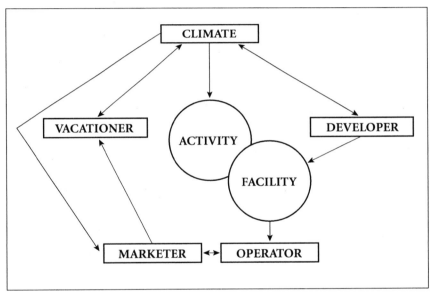

Figure 3.1: A Conceptual Framework of the Impact of Climate on Individuals Involved with the Tourism Industry.

Table 3.1: Significance to Actor of Time Horizon of Climate

TIME ACTOR	SHORT TERM (week-end)	MEDIUM TERM (year to year)	LONG TERM (10-20 years)
VACATIONER/ TOURIST	H[1]	H	L[2]
DEVELOPER	L	L	H
OPERATOR/ MARKETER	H	H	L

[1]H - high significance
[2]L - low significance

TOURISM STAKEHOLDERS – CLIMATE INTERFACE

Table 3.2 illustrates the key climate/weather components to be considered in the decision-making of each of the actors.

The Developer-Climate Interface

The developer-climate interface focuses on the long term and requires:

a)   the presence of favourable climatic conditions;
b)   the presence of ideal climate conditions for a set of tourism/recreation activities;
c)   a long and certain season of optimum climate conditions; and,
d)   the knowledge of any possible climate changes such as global warming.

Table 3.2: Climate/Weather Inputs to Tourism Stakeholders' Decision-Making

Tourism Developer	Tourism Operator/Manager
• favourable climate conditions	• advertising
• tourism/recreation activities' climate conditions	• image making
	• short-term weather/tourism conditions
• length of optimum season	
• certainty of optimum season	• weather forecasting
• climate change impact	• weather derivatives

Potential Tourist/Vacationer
• information sources
• perception/expectation
• daily weather indices
• weather forecasting

The potential participation rate in any tourism activity is conditioned by a set of variables, the most important being climate, cost and scenery (Lohmann and Kaim, 1999) together with competition from other activities and/or other locales. The highest participation rate, the tourism niche, will occur in the activity's tolerance range where variables, such as climate, are not just adequate for operation but are at their optimum (Figure 3.2). So what are the optimum/favourable climate conditions for tourism?

Because of the multivariate nature of climate, the importance of specific meteorological variables will vary with activity, gender, age and health. Yet, most researchers use temperature, wind, humidity and sunshine, either singly or in combination. Of the factors

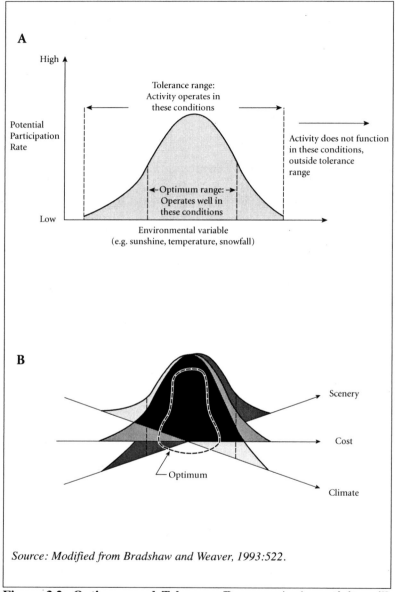

A

High ↑

Potential
Participation
Rate

Tolerance range:
Activity operates in
these conditions

Activity does not function
in these conditions,
outside tolerance
range

←Optimum range: →
Operates well in
these conditions

Low

Environmental variable
(e.g. sunshine, temperature, snowfall)

B

Scenery

Cost

Optimum

Climate

Source: Modified from Bradshaw and Weaver, 1993:522.

**Figure 3.2: Optimum and Tolerance Ranges.   A. An activity will
operate best where the environmental conditions fall within its optimum range. B. The activity's environment is in reality a set of inter-
acting variables of which climate is one.**

affecting optimum tourism climate conditions, the most important is comfort, which is either indicated by an index of body-atmosphere thermal state or more simply by temperature. It would appear that Thornes' (1977:261) "weatherless" day would represent a "good" summer holiday climatic condition of comfort, namely, "warm, dry, bright but overcast, little or no wind, excellent visibility and not too humid."

Lohmann and Kaim (1999:58) German respondents would agree but would prefer "blue skies and a lot of sunshine" to bright but overcast. Although these phrases are understood by us all, they are difficult to quantify. The result is that researchers favour unitary indices that combine variables with different weightings to determine the climate capability or climate suitability of a location for tourism. Such unitary indices are easily understood and can be used to compare locations.

A sample of indices used to indicate the climatic suitability of a site for tourism is the following:

- Effective Temperature Index (Houghten and Yaglou, 1923);
- Temperature-Humidity Index or the Discomfort Index (Thom, 1959);
- Optimum Summer Index (Davis, 1968);
- Meteorological Rating (Gaffrey, 1976);
- Humidex (Masterton and Richardson, 1979);
- Apparent Temperature or Heat Index (Steadman, 1984);
- Tourism Climate Index (Mieczkowski, 1985); and,
- Climate Index (Becker, 2000).

The Tourism Climate Index (TCI) by Mieczkowski was originally conceptualized to assess the climatic element most relevant to the quality of the tourism experience for the "average" tourism (*i.e.*, the most common tourism activity of sight-seeing and shopping

(Jansen-Verbeke, 2001)). It is the index that developers should consider because it indicates a locale's climatic suitability for the majority of tourists. The TCI is a composite index of five subindices combined from seven climate variables (Table 3.3). The TCI equals 2[4CID+CIA+2P+25+W], where the daytime comfort index is weighted at 40 per cent; precipitation and sunshine are both weighted at 20 per cent; and the daily comfort index and wind have a weighting each of 10 per cent. The TCI has a range of –24 to 100, which is divided into 11 categories. The five of greatest interest, from a tourism climate perspective, are those where the TCI is judged to be "acceptable" (50-59); "good" (60-69); "very good" (70-79); "excellent" (80-89) and "ideal" (90-100).

Theoretically, the tourism climate resource of every location can be classified into one of six annual TCI distributions (Figure 3.3). The spectrum runs from the "optimal" year-round tourism climate (TCI rating of 80 or above for each month of the year) through to a "poor" year-round tourism climate (TCI rating under 40 throughout the year). The "summer" and "winter peak" curves have similar distributions, but are distinguished by the season in which the higher TCI scores occur. The "summer peak" curve is indicative of many mid- to high-latitude locations where summer is the most pleasant period of the year for tourism. On the other hand, the "winter peak" curve represents more equatorial and mid-latitude locations where cooler and/or lower humidity conditions in winter are more comfortable for tourists compared to hot and/or humid summer conditions. Where spring and fall periods are more acceptable to the tourist, a "bimodal" or "shoulder peak" distribution is obtained. The tourism climate resource in regions with distinct wet and dry seasons will be determined to a large extent by precipitation. The TCI in these regions will display a dry season peak, when the climate is more conducive to tourism activity. Optimal, summer and winter peak distributions for various North American cities using a modified TCI are illustrated in Figure 3.4 (Scott and McBoyle, 2001).

Table 3.3: Sub-indices Within the Tourism Climate Index

Sub-Index	Monthly Climate Variables	Influence on TCI	Weighting in TCI
Daytime Comfort Index (CID)	maximum daily temperature and minimum daily relative humidity	Represents thermal comfort when maximum tourist activity occurs.	40%
Daily Comfort Index (CIA)	mean daily temperature and mean daily relative humidity	Represents thermal comfort over the full 24 hour period, including sleeping hours.	10%
Precipitation (P)	total precipitation	Reflects the negative impact that this element has on outdoor activities and holiday enjoyment.	20%
Sunshine (S)	total hours of sunshine	Rated as positive for tourism, but acknowledged can be negative because of the risk of sunburn and added discomfort on hot days.	20%
Wind (W)	average wind speed	Variable effect depending on temperature (evaporative cooling effects in hot climates rated positively, while 'wind chill' in cold climates rated negatively).	10%

Source: Scott and McBoyle, 2001.

But how valid is the modified TCI for developers in the tourism market place? Accommodation cost curves, regardless of price per night, resemble the TCI curves for the cities examined (Figure 3.5). Minor variations occur. The slight rise in summer accommodation rates at most Los Angeles hotels/resorts (Figure 3.5), despite a concurrent drop in TCI scores, may be attributed to increased demand during the school holiday period of July and August. The "low sea-

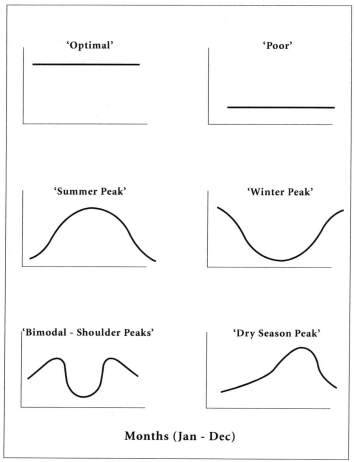

Figure 3.3: Conceptual Tourism Climate Distributions.
Source: Scott and McBoyle, 2001.

son" troughs in the accommodation cost curves near Miami are offset slightly from the TCI curve, extending up to two months longer
in the fall season when TCI curves have already begun to rise.
Overall there is some validation in the marketplace for the modified
TCI (Scott and McBoyle, 2001).

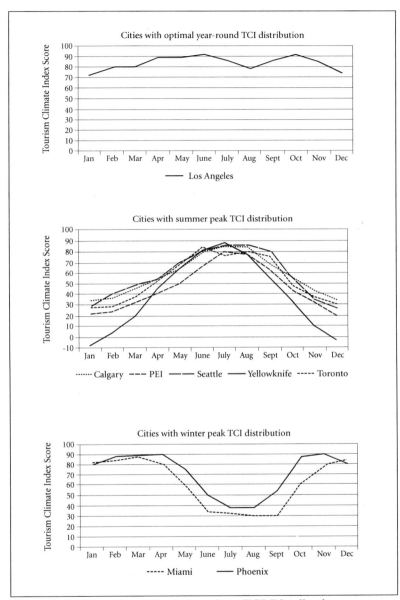

Figure 3.4: Example of North American TCI Distributions.
Source: Scott and McBoyle, 2001.

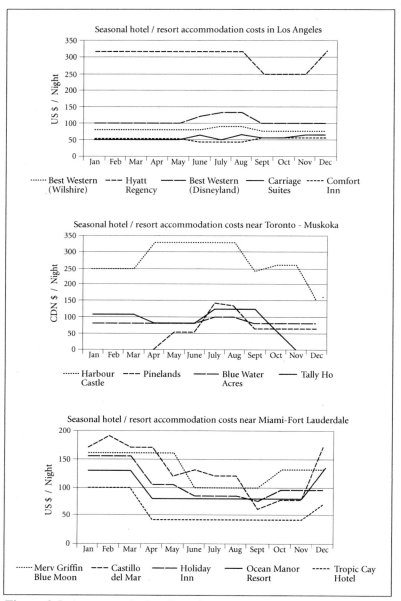

Figure 3.5: Accommodation Cost Curves.
Source: Scott and McBoyle, 2001.

The main piece of information now needed from the tourism developer's point of view is the length of time during the year when the TCI has a rating of greater than 50 – the lowest value of the "acceptable" range for tourism. In other words, there is need to determine the threshold levels, *i.e.*, the outer limits of the optimum area of the tolerance curve (Figure 3.2), beyond which participation and patronage of an activity and resort are affected negatively (Hobbs, 1980).

Other climate indices, which have a major impact on tourism, where the threshold values have been well researched and understood and accepted by the public are ultraviolet (UV) indices, which focus on protection from sunburn and skin cancer, and air pollution indices, whose values are related to health effects. The Canadian UV Index has a range of values from zero to nine plus. If the rating is seven or above, judged to be high or extreme UV, most people will "burn" within 20 minutes or less if no protection is taken. Although a tan is still an essential ingredient of a holiday to many, sunburn is a major concern to mothers when on holiday with children (Limb and Spellman, 2001).

Although rain and the lack of wind (horizontal and vertical) are judged critical for such recreation activities as hill walking (George, 1993), sailing (Houghten, 1993) and hot-air ballooning (Samuel, 1972), overall, temperature has the greatest influence on tourism/recreation participation rates. Figure 3.6 from Paul (1972) demonstrates some of the key temperature values for participation in different outdoor recreation activities.

For golf, tennis and special site visiting the participation rate peaks at a daily maximum temperature of 24°C with little participation below 10°C and a drop-off when the maximum temperature reaches 27°C and above. Hatt and McBoyle (1992) determined that 95 per cent of Waterloo Region's golfers perceived an "ideal" golfing day as one that should have average daily temperatures in the

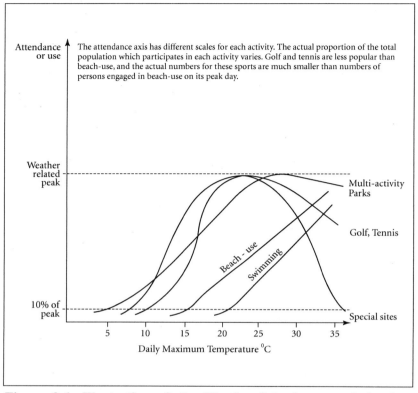

The attendance axis has different scales for each activity. The actual proportion of the total population which participates in each activity varies. Golf and tennis are less popular than beach-use, and the actual numbers for these sports are much smaller than numbers of persons engaged in beach-use on its peak day.

Figure 3.6: Illustration of the Weather-Selectiveness of Outdoor Recreationists.
Source: Paul, 1972.

range of 17 to 28°C. On the other hand, swimming and beach-use show an increasing participation rate above 21°C and are strongly favoured above 27°C (Paul, 1972). Unfortunately Paul did not define an upper thermal threshold for these activities (Smith, 1993).

In Ontario, Crowe *et al.* (1977) used climate variables to define recreation activity days *e.g.*, a "ski day" or a "beaching day" (Table 3.4). It is of significance that the thermal threshold defined for a "beaching day" by Crowe *et al.* (1977), 69°F (20.6°C) on the humidex scale (the humidex is a composite of temperature and relative humidity measuring the temperature as an individual would feel it – the "apparent" temperature) is very close to the 21°C determined by Agnew and Palutikof (2001) as the optimum summer temperature international tourists wish to find at their destination resort.

Table 3.4: Tourist/Recreation Thresholds - Climatic Criteria

Crowe *et al*. 1977:	
Beaching	- greater than 69°F (20.6°C) on the humidex scale - visibility greater than 1 mile - thick cloud less than 7/10s - hourly windspeed less than 15 mph - no measurable precipitation
Skiing	- temperature greater than 6°F (-14.4°C) - visibility greater than 0.5 miles - hourly wind speed less than 15 mph - new depth at 7 am greater than 1 inch (25 cms) - no measurable precipitation or light snow
Scott *et al*. 2002:	
Skiing	- maximum temperature of less than 10°C - less than 20 mm of liquid precipitation in 2 days - a natural snow depth of 30 cms (12 inches) or greater

Recently Scott *et al*. (2002) have redefined a "ski day" based on consultations with recreation experts and industry stakeholders, to more clearly represent climate thresholds from an industry perspective. These criteria are: a maximum temperature of less than 10°C; less than 20 mm of liquid precipitation in two days; and a natural snow depth of 30 cms or greater. Researchers of the European ski industry also take an economic perspective by defining an acceptable ski season as one in which there are 100 operable days (König, 1998). Using such criteria and the suggested climate thresholds facility developers can determine the average annual season length for various tourism activities.

What is the certainty of the season lengths? To obtain an appreciation of the interannual variation the climate data can be massaged into another form such as an index of variability or a return period.

An index of variability determines variation as a percentage of a data set's median while a return period indicates the occurrence of meeting a climate threshold, X°C, or what climate threshold will be met with a return period of once in Y years. Naturally a tourism developer is looking for locations where the index of variability and the return period are low. Neither approach has been used in the tourism/climate literature to my knowledge.

The value of the index of variability is calculated by the formula:

Index of Variability = <u>Quartile Deviation</u> x 100%
                                       Median

where the

Quartile Deviation = <u>Interquartile Range</u>
                                    2

Table 3.5 calculates the index of variability for July's mean monthly temperature for Toronto Pearson International Airport, which has a median temperature for 1976 to 1995 of 20.9°C, close to Agnew and Palutikof's 21°C summer optimum temperature. Toronto's index of variability for July's temperature is so low (3 percent) that the median temperature value could be considered nearly certain each year and, therefore, very attractive from a business plan perspective.

Table 3.5: Index of Variability at Toronto Pearson Airport for Mean Monthly Temperature for July (1976-1995)

			Rank Order	
1995	21.9°C	1	22.9	
1994	21.5	2	22.5	
1993	21.6	3	22.3	
1992	18.0	4	21.9	
1991	21.7	5	21.7	21.65
1990	20.9	6	21.6	Upper
1989	21.5	7	21.5	Quartile
1988	22.9	8	21.5	
1987	22.5	9	21.0	
1986	21.0	10	20.9	20.9
1985	19.6	11	20.9	Median
1984	19.8	12	20.6	
1983	22.3	13	20.5	
1982	20.9	14	20.5	
1981	20.6	15	20.4	20.4
1980	20.4	16	20.4	Lower
1979	20.5	17	19.8	Quartile
1978	20.4	18	19.6	
1977	20.5	19	18.6	
1976	18.6	20	18.0	

Index Variability = $\dfrac{\text{Quartile Deviation}}{\text{Median}}$ x 100%

Quartile Deviation = $\dfrac{\text{Interquartile Range}}{2}$

$= \dfrac{\text{Upper Quartile - Lower Quartile}}{2}$

QD = $\dfrac{21.65 - 20.4}{2} = \dfrac{1.25}{2} = 0.625$

Index of Variability = $\dfrac{0.625}{20.9}$ x 100%

$= 3\%$

Scott *et al.* (2002) state that a "ski day" requires a natural snow depth threshold of 30 cms or greater. Since approximately 60 per cent of a ski resort's income occurs during the Christmas break (Danard, 1980), knowing the return period for 30 cms of natural snowfall in December at a ski resort is crucial for business. The return period for this snowfall amount (calculated on Figure 3.7) for Thunder Bay is less than two years indicating that the threshold value is almost certain to occur making ski resort investment in this area attractive for a developer.

Most scientists accept the concept that global warming will occur. The implication for tourism and tourist activities that depend on climate as a base is obvious. A warmer and wetter world may reduce or extend season length; climate variability is expected to increase; activities that have thermal thresholds will be affected. How can the tourism developer plan for such a phenomenon knowing it will occur but not knowing when? By using one or more of the following techniques – a) dynamic empirical reasoning; b) historical analogue; c) sensitivity analysis; and, d) modeling; we can get a glimpse of the future.

What is dynamic empirical reasoning (DER)? It is the logical extension within a dynamic process of an increase or decrease of a set amount of one or a group of meteorological variables. For example, what would happen to the golf industry in southern Ontario if the average summer temperature increased by 2°C? The golf season would be extended; heat stress and sunburn would increase during the peak summer months since golfers are on the course for two to four hours; the seasonal golfing pattern would become bimodal with peaks near the beginning and end of the season. The extra heat would increase evaporation resulting in greater water consumption to keep the courses green, thereby possibly lowering water tables, increasing operating costs and eventually course fees.

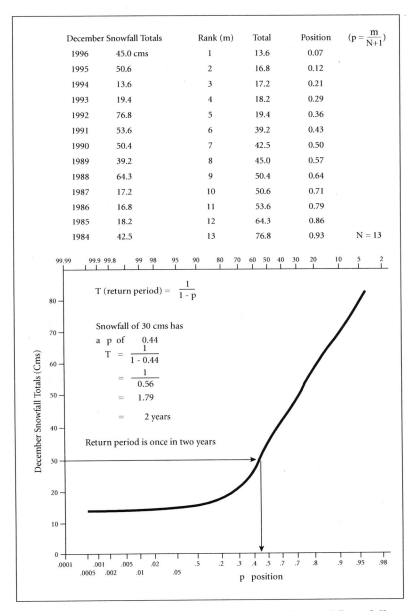

December Snowfall Totals		Rank (m)	Total	Position	$(p = \frac{m}{N+1})$
1996	45.0 cms	1	13.6	0.07	
1995	50.6	2	16.8	0.12	
1994	13.6	3	17.2	0.21	
1993	19.4	4	18.2	0.29	
1992	76.8	5	19.4	0.36	
1991	53.6	6	39.2	0.43	
1990	50.4	7	42.5	0.50	
1989	39.2	8	45.0	0.57	
1988	64.3	9	50.4	0.64	
1987	17.2	10	50.6	0.71	
1986	16.8	11	53.6	0.79	
1985	18.2	12	64.3	0.86	
1984	42.5	13	76.8	0.93	N = 13

$$T \text{ (return period)} = \frac{1}{1 - p}$$

Snowfall of 30 cms has

a p of   0.44

$$T = \frac{1}{1 - 0.44}$$

$$= \frac{1}{0.56}$$

$$= 1.79$$

$$= 2 \text{ years}$$

Return period is once in two years

Figure 3.7: Determining the Return Period of 30 cm of Snowfall at Thunder Bay for December Using the Data Set 1984 to 1996.

Maddison (2001) suggests that, for tourism in general in such countries as Greece and Spain under a temperature increase of 2°C, there will be a seasonal extension in spring and fall and flattening in summer with no overall loss in tourism numbers although Rotmans *et al.* (1996) suggest that the area suitable for sun-related tourism will decline. Perry (2001) indicates that the bimodal distribution, which he calls the "doughnut shape", reasoned for the golf season and implied by Maddison (2001), will occur in the tourist season whose summers are perceived as too hot. There does appear to be consensus in these DERs.

Braun *et al.* (1999) used a modified DER experiment to measure people's sensitivity to tourism destination choice by presenting five different scenarios indicating positive or negative climate change effects with or without reaction of the tourism industry. The respondents had no difficulty imaging the scenarios for the north German coastal region. The conclusions were that, under the climate changes presented in the scenarios, tourists would be less inclined to travel to that region than they are now. The modified DER approach indicated that tourism in that area would be impacted in the future.

The basis of the historical analogue is to use the instrumental record to obtain an anomalous period, which, by inference, could give some insight into future tourism activities and patterns because that period has similar characteristics to future climate conditions.

Giles and Perry (1998) used the summer of 1995 in the UK as an analogue year for tourism under global warming conditions since the period from June to August was the third hottest, the second driest and the fifth sunniest on record. The summer of 1995, in the UK, resulted in a dramatic increase in domestic tourism. As Giles and Perry (1998:78) state:

1995 represented a record-breaking year both for value and volume of tourism in the UK, coinciding with unusually hot weather through the year as a whole but especially the three summer months. As a result, many overseas holiday resorts were not filled, even after last-minute price reductions as holiday-makers chose to remain in the UK.

For the UK, global warming may result in revitalization of the domestic tourism market with some reduction in overseas tourism if future warmer years marry with that of 1995. Such possibilities need to be on the radar screen of tourism developers.

Scott *et al.* (2002) illustrate that, even with warm winters under global warming, the average number of potential snowmaking days per year for alpine skiing in the pre-Christmas period in the Lakelands Tourism Region of Ontario in the 2020s, and even the 2050s, will exceed those of the warm analogue years of 1982/83 and 1997/98 (Figure 3.8). This is heartening to ski resort owners in this region since it indicates that they probably will be in business in the 2050s, even under global warming conditions, if and only if they can still attract customers and operate economically while making snow at every opportunity.

How resilient to climate change is the timing and season length of set recreation activities? Is it possible for change to occur with values less than those suggested by global warming scenarios? One method of determining this is sensitivity analysis. By incrementally changing specific climate variables by a set amount, threshold values can be determined where major change in season length of an activity occurs. Using this technique it was concluded that the reduction in season length expected under global warming for alpine skiing around the Great Lakes would be obtained with a temperature increase lower than that proposed by general circulation models (Figure 3.9) McBoyle *et al.*, 1986; McBoyle and Wall,

1987; Wall, 1988; Lipski and McBoyle, 1991; McBoyle and Wall, 1992).

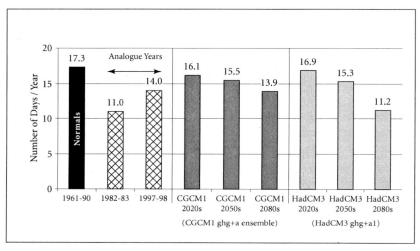

Figure 3.8: Potential Snowmaking Days (Dec. 1-20) (1961-2080s).
Source: Scott et al., 2002.

Another method a developer could use is to calculate future TCIs and recreation activity seasons by using the results of global warming modeling. Climate change scenarios were constructed for the Canadian Centre for Climatic Modelling and Analysis general circulation model (CGCM2) for the 2050s and 2080s and integrated into the modified Mieczkowski's Tourism Climate Index (TCI) for eight Canadian cities (Scott and McBoyle, 2001). The cumulative annual TCI score improved for all cities (Figure 3.10). Seasonal TCI ratings improved in each season for cities in Western Canada, making Calgary's TCI similar to present-day Denver, while the TCI rating for the summer months in Toronto and Montreal declined giving a bimodal distribution similar to that of present-day New York.

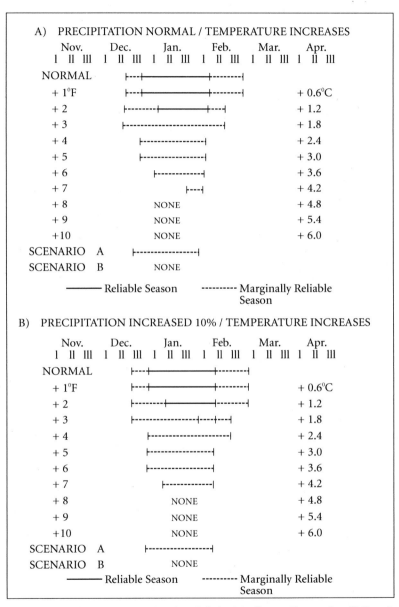

Figure 3.9: Sensitivity Analysis of Suitable Snow Cover for Skiing in the South Georgian Bay Area Using Two Sets of Criteria.

Source: McBoyle et al., 1986.

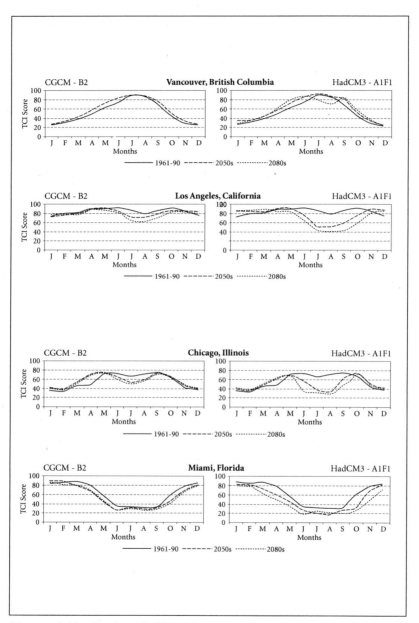

Figure 3.10: Projected Monthly Changes in TCI Rating Under Climate Change.

The future season lengths for alpine skiing, Nordic skiing and snowmobiling have been modeled, using climate thresholds, every five years until the end of this century for the Lakelands Tourism Region of Ontario (Scott *et al.*, 2002). The results indicate (Figure 3.11) that while Nordic skiing and snowmobiling will be in difficulty by the end of this decade, alpine skiing, although having a reduced season, will be kept operational with current and improved snowmaking technology if the 12 week ski season is used as the benchmark. By such modeling exercises, trends could be developed for other activities thereby giving tourism developers a glimpse of one future for a specific locale.

The Tourism Operator and Marketer-Climate Interface

There are other players in the tourism/climate arena. "Tour operators and managers plan their marketing strategies with very short horizons and claim not to incorporate climate considerations" (Agnew and Palutikof, 2001:8). What climate knowledge could be used effectively by tour operators and marketers? Advertising/image making is ubiquitous, while short-term weather/tourism relationships, forecasting and weather derivatives could be used to some advantage.

The tourism industry allocates a significant part of its budget to create desirable images of the climate at resorts – directly or indirectly – either referring in the prose to warm, sunny conditions or in the over-use of "blue sky" photography. Creating an image and an expectation is the name of the game. Obviously in tourism brochures there is scope to be selective in the presentation of climate information or to make no reference to it at all. Perry (1972), 30 years ago, said the data presented in brochures, especially for winter-time Mediterranean holidays were "misleading and evasive". Brochures often emphasized the warm winter temperature but rarely made reference to the rainfall, common in all Mediterranean locations in winter. Twenty years later, Perry (1993 and 1997) was still commenting on the fact that "misleading and incomplete

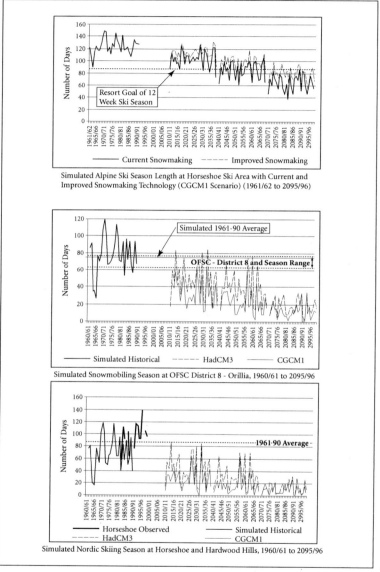

Figure 3.11: Season Lengths for Alpine Skiing, Snowmobiling and Nordic Skiing to 2095/96.

Source: Scott et al., 2002.

weather information in holiday brochures can create a false impression of a resort's climate". Recently, Maddison (2001) stated: "holiday tour operators frequently use the same "blue sky" photographs in their summer and winter brochures." Yet the 'blue sky" photography is part of deFreitas' aesthetic factor "lending light, colour, character, movement and atmosphere to scenery" as stated by Limb and Spellman (2001:7).

Smith (1993) states that expectations of visitors to Scotland may be raised by the amount of "blue sky" photography in the brochures used by the Tourist Boards. Is it surprising then that 10 per cent of British tourists and 20 per cent of foreign tourists to Scotland complain about the weather? Even Hay (1989), the director of research for VisitScotland, suggests the need for investment in indoor facilities to counter the Scottish weather. Smith (1993) suggests that the British weather could be marketed more subtlety by admitting it rains but emphasizing the weather's variety, the lack of extremes, and the role of clouds in enhancing skyscapes as felt by one of Limb and Spellman's (2001) respondents when he said:

> I think that all of us would say that we've enjoyed the experience perhaps of – not necessarily of walking in the rain but walking in the cloud – walking in overcast weather because you often see the countryside in a quite different light and certainly when I'm doing sort of higher walks the sort of broody nature of the countryside can be enhanced by cloud cover...., p.6

Tourism operators/advertisers need to be less creative and more realistic. The likelihood of a return visit to a holiday destination will be far higher if the weather the visitor/tourist expected and the weather that is actually experienced had some relationship.

Annual holidays for many people are sacrosanct. For 46 percent of the British public "having a good holiday" is their highest spending priority (Mintel, 2000). There are strong time-lapse relationships between climate and tourism participation and expenditure that are complex, difficult to explain, yet could be beneficial to the tour operator/manager when related to advertising, capacity and special discounts.

The number of British and Dutch tourists going overseas for summer holidays, for example, is influenced in part by weather conditions in their respective countries six months to a year beforehand. If the UK has a wetter than usual summer or a dull or cold winter, overseas holidays and tourism expenditures will increase the following summer (Smith, 1990; Agnew, 1995; and Giles and Perry, 1998). Using these known climate/tourism relationships, tour operators could reduce their advertising costs and discount offers and possibly increase prices because of the strong tourism demand that will be generated six to 12 months down the line.

On the other hand, in unusually hot summers, a holiday substitution effect has been noticed in parts of Europe – people taking more day trips, more short breaks and even changing annual overseas holidays to stay at home or take a domestic holiday. A summer warming of 1°C increases domestic holidays in Europe by between one and five percent (Agnew and Palutikof, 2001) while increasing domestic expenditure by four percent in Canada (Wilton and Wirjanto, 1998). With global warming, this substitution effect will probably increase. Such incipient trends need to be watched carefully by tourism operators.

Weather affects the participation rate of tourism/recreation activities. Attendance at open spaces in England is reduced by one-half that of a sunny day if the day is overcast and to one-fifth if there is continuous rain (Wager, 1967). How then does a tourist manager address the old adage: "You book your holiday depending on the climate but when you arrive there is only weather"? By posting the five-day weather forecast for the area with daily updates together with recreation activity suggestions for that day tourism managers will go a long way to address any disappointment by the tourist. If there is a possibility of rain the tourist resort personnel should recommend a visit to the local village/town (during wet days local towns prosper) rather than golf or tennis or a visit to the beach or swimming pool if the weather is forecast to be excessively hot. Naturally the resort/holiday centre with the greatest mix of activities will fare best if weather conditions change because it can minimize the tourist's dissatisfaction with the weather.

Another consideration is the emerging market of weather derivatives and weather insurance that allows tourism operators to hedge their bets against weather changes that spell the difference between profit and loss. A weather derivative is a contract between two partners that states how payment will occur as a result of poor meteorological conditions during the specified contract time (Zeng, 2000). For example, if a company wants a payment of, say $100,000 on any Friday in June that the temperature drops below 20°C, and if the probability of that happening is 10 percent, then the premium would be about $10,000. Weather derivatives, therefore, are about predicting the probability of a certain weather pattern happening or a set temperature or snowfall amount being met.

Tourism operators could cover themselves against poor weather by using weather derivatives. For example, a ski resort could establish a contract based on a specific number of days in December with adequate snowmaking temperatures or amount of snowfall; if the meteorological conditions were not met the ski area would be compensated financially. In fact, in 2000, Corney and Barrow, a chain of London (UK) wine bars set up a weather contract whereby they would receive a payment on every Thursday and Friday in summer (their most profitable days) when the temperature failed to reach 24°C (The Times, 2001).

For holiday resorts, in locales with changeable weather, weather derivatives may be good insurance. Of course, they do little for the satisfaction of the tourist!

The Tourist-Climate Interface

Because tourism is a voluntary and discretionary activity, participation will often depend on favourable climate conditions. In fact, booking an annual holiday is buying a wish fulfillment based on a location: attractiveness, climatic capability and reliability; while short-term breaks and on-holiday experiences are strongly weather dependent.

How does a potential tourist consider an area's climate capability? By means of information; perception/expectation; indices; forecasts and experience.

Travel companies' brochures are usually the first information piece obtained by the potential tourist. There are also other independent information sources – travel guides, television travel shows, travel videos and the internet (see Chapter 10). All these sources reinforce the "blue sky" photography, the comfortable, ideal and reliable weather – thereby creating a perception and generating an expectation. If an expectation is not experienced, then the level of the tourist's satisfaction and – by implication – the likelihood of a return visit is affected. However, if the climatic expectation is low, such as a visit to Scotland or Ireland, and it turns out to be "not-too-bad" weather-wise, then the weather can in fact enhance the holiday. To support this argument Paul (1972) states:

> the proportion of people who found that the weather they experienced in Ireland hindered enjoyment of their holiday was lower than the percentage who did not want to come because of the fear that the frequency of rain or the cool summer would inhibit their enjoyment.

The potential tourist may use specialist weather guides that are generally full of statistics, not easily understood and therefore rather boring. To overcome this a unitary index, such as a modified Mieckowski Tourism Climate Index (TCI) could be used – a TCI value of 80 indicating that the weather is "excellent" has meaning to a potential tourist. The TCI could be developed on a daily basis and, become as well known as the UV index, and have as great an impact as the understandable, informative weather classification presented by Besancenot *et al.* (1978) who used such terms as warm close weather, fine sunny weather, disagreeable, uncomfortable weather (Figure 3.12).

Everybody can get advice from somebody who has already visited a location. Such advice will be filtered by the on-site experience of the tourist – if adverse weather was experienced there will be strong tourist dissatisfaction; if desirable weather, comments will be favourable. Also, the potential tourist may have visited the location in previous years – this, too, will impact the likelihood of a return visit. In addition, poor weather at home within the last six to 12 months will motivate the individual to try more climatologically appealing locales.

Generally the information gathered by the potential tourist gives the perception of reliable weather. But how reliable is that perception? In Britain, for example, the second week of September normally has the most anticyclonic (warm and dry) weather of the year. However, since not everyone in Britain can take their annual holiday at that time, the potential tourist is very concerned about the weather reliability of the period chosen for the holiday. One method is to indicate the probability of good weather. For example, a location would be very attractive if the probability for the holiday period is 75 percent or higher for a TCI of at least 80. No matter the index or meteorological variable used, stating it in probability terms will be understandable and therefore informative for the potential tourist.

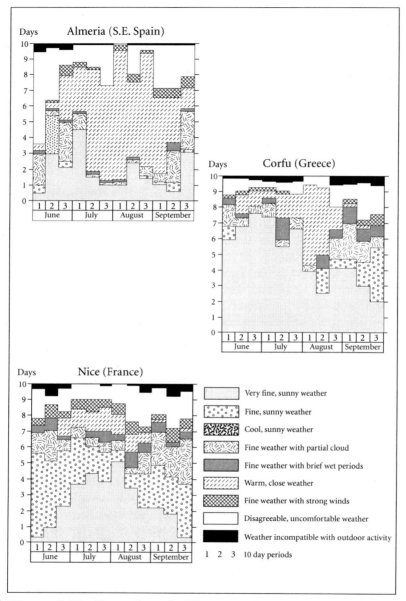

Figure 3.12: Examples of Climate Information for Tourists Produced by French Climatologists.
Source: Perry, 1993 from Besancenot et al., 1978.

Once on holiday at the location of choice, perception and expectation are replaced by reality, and weather now dominates. The daily forecast of set indices – the humidex, the UV index – dictates activities. Even some activities, such as sailing and golfing, have their own daily weather forecast on many 24 hour weather channels on television.

The substitution effect, resulting in an increase in frequency of day trips and short-term breaks, has created an "impulse" tourist since these activities are highly weather sensitive. The short-term break depends on four factors (Paul, 1972):

a)   the destination weather,
b)   the home location weather,
c)   the weather forecast, and
d)   weather conditions anticipated.

Most of these depend on the daily forecast, which, although more accurate than most people believe, has to be tempered by the commitment of the vacationer to take the break at the proposed destination (Adams, 1973). As impulse tourism increases, the weather forecast will become more important since, at least in the UK, the majority of the short breaks are being taken in the shoulder seasons when weather is very changeable.

Information and perception assist the potential tourist to make the holiday location choice while weather forecasts help to avoid on-holiday and/or short break disappointment.

CONCLUSION

Climate and weather are components of tourism. However, the knowledge of the links is still in its infancy with some relationships better understood than others. Although the knowledge base decreases from tourism developer / climate connections to tourist operators / climate-weather relationships to tourist / weather interactions (Table 3.6) there is still need for more research effort in all groups. Suggestions have been made as to how tourism developers, operators, managers, potential tourists and vacationers could make use of climate and/or weather information to assist their decision-making. How much input such suggestions have in the decision-making of the various stakeholders of tourism is relatively unknown and opens another research area.

Table 3.6: Suggested Knowledge of Climate/Weather Tourism Interactions

Tourism Developer	Knowledge Interactions (7 checks maximum)
• presence of favourable climate conditions	✔✔✔✔✔
• presence of ideal conditions for specific tourism/ recreation activities	✔✔✔
• length and certainty of optimum climate season	✔✔
• knowledge of global warming and its potential impact	✔✔
Tourism Manager/Operator	
• advertising/image making	✔✔✔✔
• short-term weather/tourism connections	✔✔✔
• weather forecasts	✔✔
• weather derivatives	✔
Potential Tourist/Vacationer	
• information sources	✔✔✔
• perception/expectation	✔
• daily weather indices	✔
• weather forecasts	✔

REFERENCES

Abegg, B., König, U., Burki, R. and Elsasser, H. (1997) "Climate impact assessment in tourism", *Die Erde*, 128:105-116.

Adams, R.L.A. (1973) "Uncertainty in nature, cognitive dissonance, and the perceptual distortion of environmental information: weather forecasts and New England beach trip decisions", *Economic Geography*, 49(4): 287-297.

Agnew, M.D. (1995) "Tourism" in J. Palutikof, S. Subak and M.D. Agnew (eds.), *Economic Impacts of the Hot Summer and Unusually Warm Year of 1995*, Department of the Environment Report, Norwich, U.K., 139-147.

Agnew, M.D. and Palutikof, J.P. (2001) "Climate impacts on the demand for tourism", in A. Matzarakis and C.R. de Freitas (eds.), *Proceedings of the First International Workshop on Climate, Tourism and Recreation*, International Society of Biometeorology, Commission on Climate Tourism and Recreation, Halkidiki, Greece, WP4, 1-10.

Anderssen, P. and Colberg, R. (1973) "Multivariate analysis in travel research: a tool for travel package design and market segmentation", *Proceedings of the Fourth Annual Travel Conference of the Travel Research Association*, 225-240.

Becker, S. (2000) "Bioclimatological rating of cities and resorts in South Africa according to the Climate Index", *International Journal of Climatology*, 20: 1403-1414.

Besancenot, J.P., Mouiner, J. and DeLavenne, F. (1978) "Les conditions climatiques du toursme litteral", *Norois*, 99: 357-382.

Bradshaw, M. and Weaver, R. (1993) *Physical Geography: An Introduction to Earth Environments*, Missouri: Mosby-York

Book, Inc.

Braun, O.L., Lohmann, M., Maksimovic, O., Meyer, M., Merkovic, A., Messerschmidt, E., Riedel, A. and Turner, M. (1999) "Potential impact of climate change effects on preferences for tourism destinations: a psychological pilot study", *Climate Research*, 11: 247-254.

Crowe, R., McKay, G. and Baker, W. (1977) *The Tourist and Outdoor Recreation Climate of Ontario, Volume 3: The Winter Season*, Downsview, ON: Atmospheric Environment Service, Environment Canada.

Danard, J. (1980) "Things look black at ski resorts – except for the white West", *The Financial Post*, January 26: 3.

Davis, N.E. (1968) "An optimum summer weather index", *Weather*, 23: 305-317.

de Freitas, C.R. (1990) "Recreation climate assessment", *International Journal of Climatology*, 10: 89-103.

de Freitas, C.R. (2001) "Theory, concepts and methods in tourism climate research", in A. Matzarakis and C.R. de Freitas (eds.), *Proceedings of the First International Workshop on Climate, Tourism and Recreation*, International Society of Biometeorology, Commission on Climate Tourism and Recreation, Halkidiki, Greece, WP 1, 1-18.

Gaffrey, D.O. (1976) "An analysis of meteorological parameters for tourism, recreation and related outdoor activities in Australia", *Paper presented to 47th ANZAAS Congress*, Hobart, Australia, 23 pages.

George, D.J. (1993) "Weather and mountain activities", *Weather*, 48: 404-410.

Giles, A.R. and Perry, A.H. (1998) "The use of a temporal analogue to investigate the possible impact of projected warming on the UK tourism industry", *Tourism Management*, 19(1): 75-80.

Harrison, S.J., Winterbotton, S.J. and Sheppard, C. (1999) "The potential effects of climate change on the Scottish tourist industry", *Tourism Management*, 20(2): 203-211.

Hatt, M. and McBoyle, G.R. (1992) "Potential impacts of global warming on the golfing season in Southern Ontario", *Paper presented at the Annual Meeting of the Association of American Geographers, East Lakes Division*, Central Michigan Univesity, Michigan.

Hay, B. (1989) "Tourism and the Scottish weather", in Harrison, S.J. and Smith, K. (eds.), *Weather Sensitivity and Services in Scotland*, Scottish Academic Press, Edinburgh, 162-166.

Hobbs, J.E. (1980) *Applied Climatology: A Study of Atmospheric Resources*, Westview Press, Dawson.

Houghten, F.C. and Yaglou, C.P. (1973) "Determining lines of equal comfort", *Transactions of the American Society of Heating and Ventilation Engineers*, 29: 163.

Houghton, D. (1993) "Winds for sailors", *Weather*, 48: 414-419.

Jansen-Verbeke (2001) "Urban tourism and tourism research", in G. Wall (ed.), *Contemporary Perspectives on Tourism*, Department of Geography Publication Series, Occasional Paper Number 17, University of Waterloo, Waterloo, Ontario, Canada, 129-142.

König, U. (1998) "Tourism in a warmer world: implications of climate change due to enhanced greenhouse effect for the ski industry in the Australian Alps", *Wirtschaftsgeographie und Raumplanung*, 28, University of Zurich, Zurich, Switzerland.

Limb, M. and Spellman, G. (2001) "Evaluating domestic tourists' attitudes to British weather: a qualitative approach", in A. Matzarakis and C.R. de Freitas (eds.), *Proceedings of the First International Workshop on Climate, Tourism and Recreation*, International Society of Biometeorology, Commission on Climate Tourism and Recreation, Halkidiki, Greece, WP2, 1-14.

Lipski, S. and McBoyle, G.R. (1990) "The impact of global warming on downhill skiing in Michigan", *East Lakes Geographer*, 26: 37-51.

Lohmann, M. (2001) "Coastal resorts and climate change", in A. Lockwood and S. Medlik (eds.), *Tourism and Hospitality in the 21st Century*, Butterworth-Heinemann, Oxford, 285-295.

Lohmann, M. and Kaim, E. (1999) "Weather and holiday destination preferences: image, attitude and experience", *The Tourist Review*, 2: 54-64.

Maddison, D. (2001) "In search of warmer climates? The impact of climate change on flows of British tourists", *Climatic Change*, 49: 193-208.

Masterton, J.M. and Richardson, F.A. (1979) *Humidex*, CLI-79, Downsview, ON: Atmospheric Environment Service, Environment Canada.

McBoyle, G.R. and Wall, G. (1987) "The impact of CO_2 induced warming on downhill skiing in the Laurentians", *Cahiers de*

Geographie du Quebec, 31: 39-50.

_____ (1992) "Great Lakes skiing and climate change", in A. Gill and R. Hartmann (eds.), *Mountain Resort Development*, Proceedings of the Vail Conference, 82-92.

McBoyle, G.R., Wall, G., Harrison, R., Kinnaird, V. and Quinlan, C. (1986) "Recreation and climatic change: a Canadian case study", *Ontario Geography*, 28: 51-68.

Mieczkowski, Z. (1985) "The tourism climatic index: a method of evaluating world climates for tourism", *The Canadian Geographer*, 29(3): 220-233.

Mintel (2000) "Holiday by lifestage", *Leisure Intelligence*, September.

Paul, A. (1972) "Weather and the daily use of outdoor recreation areas in Canada", in J.A. Taylor, D. and C. Newton Abbot (eds.), *Weather Forecasting for Agriculture and Industry*, 132-146.

Perry, A.H. (1972) "Weather, climate and tourism", *Weather*, 27: 199-203.

_____ (1993) "Climate and weather information for the package holiday-maker", *Weather*, 48: 410-414.

_____ (1997) "Recreation and tourism", in R. Thompson and A. Perry (eds.), *Applied Climatology*, Routledge, London: 240-248.

_____ (2000) "Impacts of climate change on tourism in the Mediterranean: adaptive responses", *Fonazione Eni Enrico Mattei*, Milan, Italy, Nota di Lavoro, 35.

_____ (2001) "More heat and drought – Can Mediterranean tourism survive and prosper?", in A. Matzarakis and C.R. de Freitas (eds.), *Proceedings of the First International Workshop on Climate, Tourism and Recreation*, International Society of Biometeorology, Commission on Climate Tourism and Recreation, WP3, 1-6.

Rotmans, J., Hulme, M. and Downing, T.E. (1994) "Climate change implications for Europe", *Global Environmental Change*, 4: 97-124.

Samuel, G.A. (1972) "Some meteorological and other aspects of hot-air ballooning", *Meteorological Magazine*, 101: 25-29.

Scott, D. and McBoyle, G. (2001) "Using a modified 'tourism climate index' to examine the implications of climate change for climate as a natural resource for tourism", in A. Matzarakis and C.R. de Freitas (eds.), *Proceedings of the First International Workshop on Climate, Tourism and Recreation*, International Society of Biometeorology, Commission on Climate Tourism and Research, Halkidiki, Greece, WP 6, 1-18.

Scott, D., Jones, B., Lemieux, C. McBoyle, G., Mills, B., Svenson, S. and Wall, G. (2001) *The Vulnerability of Winter Recreation to Climate Change in Ontario's Lakelands Tourism Region*, Report to Government of Canada's Climate Change Action Fund, 82 pages.

Scott, D., Jones, B., Lemieux, C. McBoyle, G., Mills, B., Svenson, S. and Wall, G. (2002) *The Vulnerability of Winter Recreation to Climate Change in Ontario's Lakelands Tourism Region*, Department of Geography Publication Series, Occasional Paper Number 18, University of Waterloo, Ontario.

Smith, K. (1990) "Tourism and climate change", *Land Use Policy*, April: 176-180.

_____ (1993) "The influence of weather and climate on recreation and tourism", *Weather*, 48: 398-404.

Steadman, R.G. (1984 "A universal scale of apparent temperature", *Journal of Climate and Applied Meteorology*, 23:1674-1687.

The Times (2001) "Hedging against the weather could save business millions", *The Times*, 16 April.

Thom, E.C. (1959) "The discomfort index", *Weatherwise*, 12(2): 57-60.

Thornes, J.E. (1977) "The effect of weather on sport", *Weather*, 32: 258-268.

Wager, J. (1967) "Outdoor recreation on common land", *Journal of the Town Planning Institute*, 53:398-403.

Wall, G. (1992) "Tourism alternatives in an era of global climate change", in V.C. Smith and V.R. Eadington (eds.), *Tourism Alternatives*, Chichester: John Wiley, 194-215.

Wall, G. (1998) "Impacts of climate change on recreation and tourism", in N. Mayer and W. Avis (eds.), *Responding to Global Climate Change – National Sectoral Issues (Volume XII) of the Canada Country Study*, Climate Impacts and Adaptation, Toronto, ON: Environment Canada, 591-620.

Wall, G. and McBoyle, G.R. (1992) "Climate change and its implications for recreation in mountain areas", in A. Gill and R. Hartmann (eds.), *Mountain Resort Development, Proceedings of the Vail Conference*, 70-81.

Wilton, D. and Wirjanto, T. (1988) *An Analysis of the Seasonal Variation in the National Tourism Indicators*, Ottawa, ON: Canadian Tourism Commission.

Winslow, C.E.A., Herrington, L.P. and Gagge, A.P. (1938) "Physiological reactions and sensations of pleasantness under varying atmospheric conditions", *Transactions of the American Society of Heating, Refrigerating and Air Conditioning Engineers*, 44:179-194.

Zeng, L. (2000) "Weather derivatives and weather insurance: concept, application, and analysis", *Bulletin of the American Meteorological Society*, 81:2075-2082.

4

Tourism in Mountainous Environments: The Mt. Everest Region of Nepal

Sanjay K. Nepal

INTRODUCTION

Mountainous regions, in most cases, are inaccessible, fragile, marginalized by political and economic decision-making, and home to one of the poorest people in the world (Messerli and Ives, 1997). Poverty is widespread, especially in the mountains of the developing countries, while remoteness, fragility and marginality often lead to extensive degradation. Mountains have been treated as peripheral regions in most countries. There are also opportunities to be tapped, however. Rich in freshwater resources, and home to a great variety of flora, and fauna and to a number of global biodiversity hot spots, mountains offer opportunities for self-development, and for development that will benefit surrounding lowland areas. Tourism development is seen as an obvious choice, and one of the means for achieving sustainable mountain development. Many mountain regions have been developed as popular travel destinations: from the Rocky Mountains in North America to the Andean Cordillera in South America; the Alps and Pyrenees in Europe; the Hindu-Kush Himalaya; from the Atlas mountains in North Africa to Drakensberg in South Africa; and the Alps in New Zealand and Australia (Mountain Agenda, 1999; Williams *et al.*, 2001).

Tourism is one of the largest industries in the world, and its growth has been impressive in recent decades. The World Tourism Organization (WTO) predicts that by the year 2010, international tourism will grow to one billion visitors a year, and account for 11.6 per cent of the global gross domestic product (WTTC, 1999). It is estimated that by 2010 approximately 250 million people will be employed in the tourism industry, and 10.6 per cent of total capital investments will be made in the tourism sector (WTTC, 1999). Although such predictions may be questioned in the light of recent international events, the significant impacts and implications of global tourism cannot be understated.

This chapter discusses the impacts of tourism on mountainous environments; the focus is on tourism-induced environmental changes. The Mt. Everest region is selected because it represents a tourism destination located in a remote and peripheral region, but significantly rich in biodiversity, and hence, sensitive to development. It is a useful case study to illustrate the challenges and opportunities for mountain development based primarily on tourism. The paper briefly introduces mountain-specific characteristics and their implications for tourism. It then provides a brief background of the study area, followed by a detailed analysis of tourism development. Four major environmental issues are examined: (i) impacts on human settlements, (ii) consumption of fuelwood and other energy sources, (ii) accumulation of garbage, and (iv) the degradation of mountain trails. A brief discussion on changes in the spatial characteristics of the region is provided, followed by some conclusions.

MOUNTAINS AND TOURISM

In general, the impact of and the issues of tourism development in the mountains are not the same in developing and developed countries. When considering mountain tourism issues, the striking differences between mountain destinations in developed countries and those in developing countries must therefore be kept in mind.

In developed countries many mountain tourist destinations have become major players in the local economy. With a relatively high volume and value, they have the characteristics of mass tourism. However, recent trends indicate a surge in visitors to eco-tourism type destinations such as remote wilderness areas, where access is only possible on foot or by air. Hiking, camping, mountain and rock climbing, mountain biking, wildlife viewing, and other forms of non-consumptive recreation are in growing demand, particularly in North America. For instance, the 1994-1995 US National Survey on recreation and the Environment reported that between 1982/83 and 1994/95, the number of bird-watchers had increased by 155 per cent, hikers by 94 per cent and backpackers by 73 per cent (US Federal Government, n.d. cited in Fennell, 2001). In European countries such as UK and Germany, the trend is towards specialized and small travel fairs developing around "green," "nature," and "sustainable tourism" concepts (Blangy and Vautier, 2001). The establishment of national parks and protected areas in several east European and central Asian countries will no doubt increase the number of visitors to this region, particularly from western Europe.

Mountain tourism destinations in developed countries are characterized by consolidation of businesses to increase profits and efficiency through reduced management costs and internal structural adjustments. But apart from these measures, strict regulations and control in the quality of services and facilities, implementation of environmental measures such as emission and pollution standards, minimization of energy costs, appropriate measures for solid waste disposal, and treatment of sewage have become focal concerns.

In contrast with mountain areas in developed countries, mountains in developing countries are often influenced by the countries' high population growth rates and characterized by inaccessibility, marginal development, peripheral locations (from a global perspective), high levels of stress on natural resources, rampant poverty, and highly skewed distribution of wealth and property. Historical developments (former colonial rule), political systems (for example, in eastern European and Central Asian countries), and issues of governance (civil wars and conflicts such as those in Central and South America) have marred efforts in mountain development. However, developing mountains are also characterized by high biological and cultural diversity. National and international efforts to conserve biodiversity in these mountains have resulted in an impressive network of national parks and protected areas. The past few decades have seen a dramatic increase in visitor numbers to areas such as the world's highest national park the Sagarmatha (Mt. Everest) National Park in Nepal, Taman Negara National Park, a highland rainforest in West Malaysia, Simen Mountains National Park in northern Ethiopia, and Huascarán National Park in Peru. Similarly, several recently established national parks and protected areas in Central Asia hope to promote tourism.

With few exceptions, the developing mountains are in their early stages of tourism development, and many destinations are marketed and promoted as ecotourism destinations. An earlier survey had indicated that 17 per cent of the North American-based eco-tour providers reported that their clients were primarily interested in traveling to Asia-Pacific mountain regions (Yee, 1992 cited in Lew 2001). If the WTO predictions hold true, Asia will experience the highest growth rate in visitor arrivals and receipts (WTO, 1998). A potentially positive trend in the 1990s has been a growth in domestic and intra-Asian tourism (Ghimire, 2000). Recent reports have also indicated that despite the global slump on international arrivals, triggered by the events of September 11, several Asian countries mantained its arrival numbers (CTC, 2003). This clearly indicates a significant growth potential for mountain tourism in Asia. Domestic tourism is also on the rise in South America. The Andean highlands, notably in Ecuador, Peru, and Argentina are considered strong mountain tourism destinations in South America.

Tourism in the developing mountains is characterized by haphazard planning, lack of environmental standards and monitoring, price cutting resulting in high volume and low returns, stark seasonality, and domination of tourism in the overall economy. Some of the problems of tourism in developing mountains include competition between small-scale local operations and large international chains, alienation of local residents as a result of large number of visitors, sharp rises in property values, environmental damage, and native inhabitants being confronted with the values of post-industrial society (Stone, 1992; Nepal, 1999).

Mountains in general, have certain characteristics that make them unique compared to other eco-regions. These specific characteristics have significant implications on the type, scale, and extent of tourism development (Table 4.1). For example, difficult access in the mountains translates to limited range of tourism opportunities; however, this could mean that mountain tourism entrepreneurs can take advantage of the relative inaccessibility and develop a high quality and high value tourism product. The fragile characteristics of the mountains restrict tourism development to areas that are resilient, while micro-variations in physical and biological attributes imply the development of location-specific tourism product. In other words, site-specific characteristics largely dictate the type of development of tourism services and facilities. Thus, each region will have its own tourism niche, which should be duly considered when marketing the destination. Finally, mountain tourism destinations will have to consider their marginality, in terms of political and economic powers, to influence policy and decision-making that could affect local level tourism developments. This usually means tourism development in mountain regions have to be based on the local capacity to plan, develop and manage tourism resources, with as little outside help as possible.

The Everest region exhibits all the characteristics mentioned above. It is located in a remote place, and is not accessible by vehicular traffic. Its environment is extremely fragile: high altitude, sharp variations in relief, extreme climate, and tectonic activities that frequently trigger natural hazards, make the region ecologically vulnerable. The region is supported by rich flora and fauna, and is also at the crossroads of different cultures such as the Tibetan culture of the highland areas and the cultures introduced by more recent emi-

Table 4.1: Characteristics of Mountainous Regions and Implications for Tourism

Main Characteristics	Attributes	Implications for Tourism
Difficult access	Remoteness Isolation from markets Insular economy and culture	High value Activities that take advantage of relative inaccessibility
Fragility	Resources vulnerable to rapid degradation	Niche tourism Employment in environmental conservation Restricted use of biological hotspots Carrying capacity considerations
Diversity	Micro variations in physical and biological attributes Interdependence of production bases	Use of specific comparative advantage Linkage with local production systems Small-scale technological innovation Revival of traditional activities
Niche	Location-specific attractions Endemic flora and fauna Area-specific resources/production activities	Special interest tourism Niche marketing Skill-based or culturally specific crafts Area-specific tourist goods and services
Marginality	Limited local resources Marginal concern to decision-makers Unfavourable terms of trade	Optimal/judicious use of tourism resources Local-level, participatory decision-making Mandatory reinvestment of tourism revenues Institutional capacity and manpower development Monitoring mechanism

Source: Sharma (2000) cited in Nepal et al., 2002: 13.

grants to the region. Specific attributes such as high mountains, scenic landscapes, Buddhist monasteries and Tibetan culture, and endemic wildlife make this region particularly attractive for those seeking adventure tourism. The Mt. Everest region offers unparalleled mountaineering and trekking opportunities. Since historical times, the Sherpa people have managed natural resources based on indigenous systems. Because the region is far away from the administrative center in Kathmandu, except for the purposes of collecting taxes hardly any outsiders considered traveling to the region, until it was discovered by foreign mountaineers. Without the development of tourism, it is likely this region would have faced the same fate as its neighboring districts where poverty and underdevelopment are widespread. The lack of government intervention in the region was perhaps a primary factor to motivate local people to develop their own strategies for economic development and resource conservation. The following section provides a brief background of the study area.

THE STUDY AREA

Located in the northeastern highlands of Nepal, along the Nepal-China border, the Sagarmatha National Park's (SNP) 1150 km^2 area is a World Heritage Site. It consists of rugged landscape of high mountains, glaciers, hanging valleys and constricted fluvial terraces, and is dissected by four main valleys: Bhote Koshi in the west, Dudh Koshi in the central, and Imja Khola with its two forks namely Lobuche Khola and Imja Khola proper, in the east (Figure 4.1). The Park can be broadly divided into three vegetation zones based on altitude: the lower altitudinal belt (below 3800 meters) consisting of temperate forests and woodlands; the middle zone (3800 – 4200 meters) of sub alpine forests and shrub land; and the upper zone (above 4200 meters) of tundra vegetation. The soils in the high valleys are primarily Entisols, with shallow depths of less than 65 centimeters. Below 4000 meters, Spodosols have developed in forested areas, which are mainly located in the north-facing slopes. The extensive grassland and shrubland areas, mainly in the southern slopes below 3750 meters have Inceptisol and Entisol soils (Byers, 1987). The climate in the Park ranges between temperate to arctic conditions, depending on altitude and aspect. The mean daily temperature recorded at Namche Bazaar (3400 m), where the park headquarter is located, is -0.4°C in January and 12°C in July. Precipitation is highly seasonal, peaking during the period between June and September, and varies regionally with local topographic conditions (Garratt, 1981).

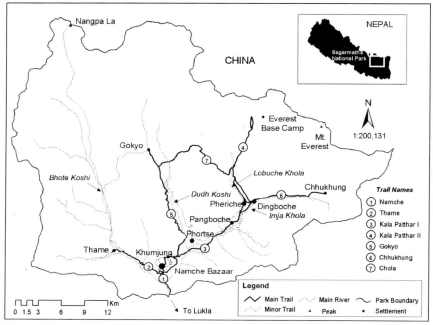

Figure 4.1: Location of the Study Area.

The Park supports rich wild animal populations and bird species. Most commonly sighted animals are the Himalayan Thar (*Hemitragus jemlahicus*) - a species of wild goat, and Musk Deer (*Moschus moschiferus*). At least 118 bird species are found in the Park, which include resident and migrant birds. It is also home to the Impeyan pheasant (*Lophophorus impejanus*), the national bird of Nepal. Jefferies (1985) provides details of the animal and bird species found in the Park.

The *Sherpa*, present day inhabitants, are believed to have migrated from an eastern province in Tibet some four centuries ago (Jefferies, 1982). Originally nomads, Sherpa began to settle permanently after the introduction of potato in 1850 while maintaining transhumance migration (Bjønness, 1980). Today, the Everest region is home also to a small population of other ethnic groups such as the *Rai* and *Tamang* from the neighboring highlands, and *Brahmin*, *Chetri* and *Newar* from the lowlands. Namche Bazaar, the heartland of Khumbu, has a cosmopolitan atmosphere where visitors from all over the world could be met. The main settlements within the Park are Namche Bazaar, Khumjung, Khunde, Phortse, Pangboche, Thamicho, Pheriche and Dingboche. There are as many as 60 other subsidiary settlements, mostly herding villages (Stevens, 1993), some of which have been transformed to permanent or semi-permanent tourist villages. All the settlements are technically excluded from the Park.

The Park is visited every year by more than 25,000 trekkers and mountaineers from around the world. The majority of trekkers stay in local lodges, while some of those on organized trekking and mountaineering expeditions prefer to stay in tents. There are around 155 lodges, which are located strategically along the major trekking routes (Nepal *et al.*, 2002). When the number of guides and porters, and other support staff are combined, total annual visitors to the Park could reach anywhere between 40,000 and 50,000. This is a significant number considering that the total resident population within the Park is less than 3,200.

TOURISM-INDUCED ENVIRONMENTAL CHANGES

This section discusses the effects of tourism on human settlements, fuelwood and energy, garbage accumulation, and the degradation of trails.

Human Settlements

Although tourism evolved in the early 1950s, it was not until the early 1970s that the first lodge was built. Trekking tourism started in Everest with 20 trekkers arriving in 1964. It is reasonable to assume that since the number of trekkers and mountaineers were few, lodging did not make a viable business at that time. Indeed, until 1978, 70 per cent of the trekkers to the Everest region were part of the organized tour who stayed out in camps (Bjønness,

1980). Owing to the steady growth in visitor numbers and the increase in independent trekkers, lodge accommodation started to become a viable business, and many lodges were constructed during the 1980s. The 1990s saw an astonishing growth in number of lodges, with over 64 per cent of the total lodges in the Everest region being opened during this period.

A comparison of some selected settlements along the main trails provides some interesting observations with respect to lodge development over time (Table 4.2). Namche Bazaar and Lukla are the main settlements with a higher concentration of lodges, which together constitute 25 per cent of all lodges in the Everest region. In the second order are Phakding, Pangboche, Dingboche, and Pheriche with 20 per cent of all lodges. In terms of growth over time, lodges in Namche, Lukla, and Phakding have grown considerably, while in Monjo/Jorsalle, Pangboche, and Dingboche, lodges increased mainly until 1993/94. Phortse, Gokyo, Pheriche, and Thame have shown steady growth even if the total number of lodges is much lower. The proportionate shares of Lukla and Namche show a declining trend, while for other areas the trend is increasing but at a slower rate. This indicates two important findings. First, lodge development in the more established villages has slowed down, with the implication that the accommodation capacity in these villages has reached its peak. Secondly, partly due to higher concentration of lodges and corresponding accommodation capacity in these established villages, new lodges are being constructed in other smaller villages.

Table 4.2: Cumulative Growth of Lodges in Selected Settlements*

Settlements	Until 1989/90		Until 1993/94		After 1995	
	Lodge	%	Lodge	%	Lodge	%
Everest	86	100.0	161	100.0	225	100.0
Lukla	12	14.0	19	11.8	23	10.2
Phakding	6	7.0	9	5.6	13	5.8
Monjo/Jorsalle	5	5.8	7	4.3	8	3.6
Namche Bazaar	16	18.6	26	16.1	33	14.7
Thame	3	3.5	5	3.1	9	4.0
Phortse	2	2.3	3	1.9	5	2.2
Gokyo	1	1.2	5	3.1	8	3.6
Pangboche	3	3.5	8	5.0	10	4.4
Dingboche	4	4.7	9	5.6	10	4.4
Pheriche	3	3.5	5	3.1	10	4.4

*Per centile figures for individual settlements are calculated from the total number of lodges in each region.
Source: Adapted from Nepal (1999), p.60.

Tourism-induced growth in lodge accommodation has intro-duced significant changes in settlement and housing patterns and has led to the expansion of built up areas. Lodge construction has indeed been a booming business in the last 20 years and is clearly linked to independent trekking, which became increasingly impor-tant from the late 1960s onwards; contrary to group treks or moun-taineering expeditions, independent trekkers do not carry tents and therefore depend on overnight facilities. In 1980, the total number of lodge accommodations was 17, and in 1997 225, representing a 13-fold increase between 1980 and 1997 in the region (Table 4.3). Lodge construction appears to continue unabated, and in November 1997, building sites could be found in almost every village in the Everest region.

Table 4.3: Growth in Numbers of Visitors and Lodges

Year	Number of Tourists	Number of Lodges	Number of Settlements with Lodges
1980	5,836	17	12
1990	7,950	75	29
1997	18,200	225	38

Source: Nepal et al. (2002), p.39.

The village of Namche Bazaar exemplifies the tourism-induced growth of settlements and changes in character of rural settlements. Based on the aerial photographs taken in 1955 and 1982, series of ground photos taken during the last three decades, and several photographs and field sketch prepared in 1997, it is feasible to examine the expansion of the built up area, and changes in the utility of the buildings (Figure 4.2). Between 1955 and 1997, the built-up areas doubled owing to the construction of new houses and lodges. The village has expanded into the less sunny slopes of the valley it occupies, as well as onto the plain above it. This area is less protected against the wind, and for this reason was not developed in the past. The number of inhabitants increased from 296 in 1957 to 1328 in 1997. A new village center dominated by lodges and shops has emerged, and building density has increased considerably. In 1997, for example, Namche Bazaar was visited by about 18,000 trekkers and mountaineers. At this time, there were 33 lodges with a total of over 800 beds while only four lodges existed around 1980. Namche's shopping mile has an urban, cosmopolitan touch, unknown in other, much bigger, settlements in Nepal. Namche Bazaar has a range of German and Swiss bakeries, laundry services, video halls and internet cafés. At least one lodge is equipped with an elevator, while two banks and a large number of shops with an impressive range of imported consumer goods – including mountaineering equipment, clothing, food, and local and Tibetan curios – serve the burgeoning tourist population.

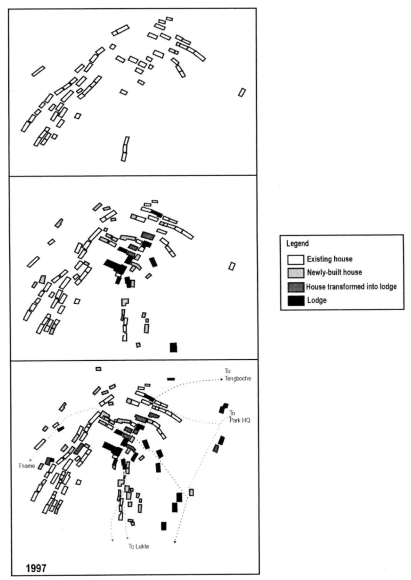

Figure 4.2: Expansion of Namche Bazaar Between 1955 and 1997.

Source: Nepal, 2002, p. 785.

Currently, there is a declining trend in constructing new lodges in the major settlements of Namche Bazaar and Lukla. This may imply that lodge construction in these villages has saturated, whereas in other areas it is an on-going activity. A fundamental shift in settlement patterns, utilization of physical space, and land use changes are bound to occur if the rate of development proceeds unchecked. The implication of significant housing construction is that there has been tremendous pressure on local forests for timber supply and fuelwood requirements.

Fuelwood and Energy
Of all the environmental issues concerning the Himalaya, the state of the forests and reports about their destruction have undoubtedly received the widest attention among scientists, administrators, tourists, and the environmentally conscious public in many parts of the world. It cannot be denied that population growth has led to an increasing demand for timber used in construction as well as for fuelwood. Wood is the principal source of energy in the Nepalese Himalaya, and tourism has created additional demand for it in the main tourist centers such as the Everest region. There have been considerable debates on the accuracy and reliability of deforestation reports in the region, and this is certainly beyond the scope of the discussion here, as it focuses only on the effects of tourism (Byers, 1987; Ives and Messerli, 1990; Nepal *et al.*, 2002)

A 1997 survey conducted among the lodges within the Everest region indicated that a total of 4.65 tons of fuelwood were burned daily by the 155 lodges operating within the Park boundary. This roughly translates to 30 kilograms of fuelwood per lodge. If all lodges and private households are added together, annual fuelwood consumption in the villages within the Park amounts to 4,014 tons. Twenty-one per cent of this is consumed by the lodges, a figure which confirms past estimates (Table 4.4). Overall, private household consumption in Khumbu is about four times higher than in the tourism sector.

Table 4.4: Share of Tourism in Fuelwood Consumption

Items	Consumption in Metric Tons or %
Annual consumption, all lodges	
Tourist season (180 days)	837 t
Off-season (180 days)	418 t
Annual consumption,	
All other households (365 days)	2759 t
Total consumption	4014 t
Share of lodges in total consumption	21 %
Estimate in Pawson et al. (1984)	10 %
Estimate in Hardie (1987)	20 %

Source: Nepal et al., 2002, p.43.

Some reservations must be added to the above estimates. First, the estimates only include fuelwood consumption by lodges; other tourism-related demands, such as the demands for porters, are not considered. Porters do not influence overall fuelwood consumption in a larger regional context – they cook their dish or rice twice a day as they do at home. However, their presence in tourist regions increases the overall local consumption of fuelwood. Second, these calculations represent averages. In the main tourist centers the share of tourism is undoubtedly much higher. In Namche Bazaar, the tourist hub in the Everest region, it has been estimated that tourism-induced fuelwood consumption equals, or exceeds, consumption by private households (Stevens, 1993). Many lodges collect their fuelwood and buy construction timber from forests outside the national park, particularly from the Pharak region, which is situated below the Park. The establishment of the Park has thus led to increased pressure on forests in adjacent areas. As a consequence, the Pharak area, and especially villages located close to the Park such as Monjo, Jorsalle and Phakding, have become major fuelwood and timber supply centers for the main tourist locations in the Park. Nonetheless, illegal cutting, especially of young trees and brushes, is widespread inside the Park, particularly near tourist centers and in alpine areas above the forests. As a result, high altitude juniper forests are more severely affected by tourism than the montane forest, particularly along the upper parts of the main trail to the Everest Base Camp (Byers, 2002). As a result, dung is now widely used as a fuel at higher altitudes. In 1997, 34 per cent of all lodges above 4,000 meters used dung as their main source of energy (Mattle, 1997). It should be mentioned here that the national park rules prescribe that trekking groups use only alternative energy sources such as kerosene or gas for cooking, while Park staff and the various units of the Nepalese Army deployed in the region have continued to use fuelwood, generally cut inside the Park.

Although significant progress has been made in alternative fuel energy sources, their adoption as cooking fuel lags far behind the increased levels of fuelwood consumption, primarily because fuelwood is still the cheapest source of energy and in most areas easily available. On the average, the price of fuelwood is about five times lower per unit of energy than that of kerosene or gas (Nepal *et al.*, 2002). It can be collected free of charge, and is still obtained relatively easily in many places. Where it is scarce and thus more expensive, as in remote and high altitude settlements above the timberline, lodge owners choose alternative energy sources.

Since January 1995, about 600 households from eight villages have received electricity from the small hydropower plant in Thame. After one year of operation, capacity utilization at the plant reached 60 per cent. Actual electricity consumption data showed that ordinary households and teashops consumed 70 per cent of the electricity and contributed 72 per cent of electricity revenues. Fuelwood was still the single most important source of energy for the households connected to the power grid. Ninety-two per cent of all households used wood for their energy needs, often in combination with dung. However, 77 per cent also consumed electricity, while nine per cent burned kerosene or gas in addition. Thus, many households relied on more than one energy source, and only eight per cent of all households indicated that they relied solely on electricity. Overall, the introduction of electricity reduced fuelwood consumption by 30 per cent, *i.e.*, from 30 kg to 20 kg on average per day and household (Fischbacher, 1999). Electricity has thus been well accepted by the local community, but there is significant potential for greater reduction of fuelwood consumption, especially in lodges.

Garbage Accumulation

Garbage pollution in the Nepalese Himalaya has been a concern since the late 1980s. Local and international media have highlighted this issue. Some of the garbage-related statements are exaggerated, but the severity of the problem is real, especially in the Everest region.

The garbage data prepared by SPCC indicates that, on average, there is almost two tons of garbage per kilometer of a tourist trail. In terms of the amount of garbage, Namche tops the list with over 12 tons per kilometer, followed by Thame with almost a ton of garbage (Table 4.5). Although with far less volume per kilometer, Kala Patthar, and Chhukhung are in the third order, and Gokyo and Chola have the least amount of garbage. It is interesting to note that with the exception of Thame, amount of garbage, visitor and packstock traffic, and lodge density follow similar patterns, for example, Namche has the highest amount of garbage, highest visitor and packstock traffic, and highest lodge density. This is also true, with a little variation, for Kala Patthar, Chhukhung, Gokyo and Chola trails.

Table 4.5: Indicators of Trail Use Intensity

Trail	Trail Length	Garbage (ton/km)	Trail Use Intensity (per kilometer per day)		Lodge (per km)
	(km)		Visitor	Pack Stock	
Namche	14.0	12.14	14.4	1.2	3.3
Thame	9.2	0.89	5.2	1.8	1.0
Kala Patthar I	17.9	0.25*	7.3	0.5	2.5
Kala Patthar II	16.6		6.7	0.2	0.7
Gokyo	20.4	0.08	4.0	0.2	1.1
Chhukhung	4.5	0.11	7.6	0.3	0.9
Chola	6.6	0.02	6.3	0.0	0.3

*Including Kala Patthar II.
Source: Garbage data (SPCC, 1997); Trekkers data (Nepal, 1999).

The total volume of garbage has been increasing every year, even though the number of climbing expeditions has decreased in recent years (Nepal, 1999). Trekking-related garbage now far exceeds expedition garbage. Indeed, it is an irony that the accumulation of garbage has encouraged a new type of tourism, *i.e.*, garbage clean up expeditions, and has also provided employment opportunities to local people. Since 1994, the Sagarmatha Pollution Control Committee (SPCC), a *Sherpa* run NGO based in Namche Bazaar, has been involved in solid waste management. The organization hires people who collect and sort the garbage; papers and other disposables are burned, and recyclable items such as beer bottles, tins, and batteries are sent to Kathmandu for recycling. More recently, local authorities have banned the import of bottled drinks. Similarly, a local mineral water plant has been using recycled plastic bottles. Overall, efforts in solid waste management have been encouraging, but hinge on continued support from the government, local communities, tourists, and foreign donors. Recycling has been a problem, however, as there is no recycling plant in the region, and everything that needs to be recycled has to be flown out of the region. This makes garbage management in the region a formidable challenge and an expensive job.

Trail Degradation

Another significant environmental issue but one that has received very little attention, is the impact of tourism on trail degradation. Since trekking is the main form of tourism, trails are a crucial element of tourism infrastructure. One of the purposes of the trail survey was to examine if there was any correlation between visitor use, and the magnitude and extent of impacts. Visitor and packstock surveys were conducted for three months during the period between September and December 1997 (Nepal, 1999). These are interpreted in terms of number of visitors on a kilometer of a trail on any given day, during the peak tourist season between September and December. Lodge counts were completed during the same period. Data on trail use intensity indicate that Namche has the highest visitor and packstock traffic (refer to Table 4.5). There are more lodge accommodations along the Namche trail, followed by Kala Patthar I, and are evenly distributed along the Thame, Gokyo, and Chhukhung trails.

A detailed survey of trail conditions was conducted in 1997 to check the severity of trail degradation. Data on 12 different types of impact features were collected. These include trail incision, exposed soil, exposed bedrock, trail width, multiple treads, trail expansion potential, trail displacement, landslide scar, running water, muddiness, root exposure, and the absence of ground litter (Nepal, 1999). Based on the measurements of the individual impact features, trails were grouped into four categories, namely: very little damage (Class I), moderately damaged (Class II), highly damaged (Class III), and severely damaged (Class IV). Results indicate that there are 69 Class I, 58 Class II, 16 Class III, and 65 Class IV trails. About 44 per cent of the total length of the Park trails (89.1

km) is degraded in one form or another (Table 4.6). The total length
of Class I is 12.4 km, Class II 10 km, Class III 3.4 km, and Class IV
11.6 km.

Table 4.6: Trail Assessment Based on Condition Class System (figure in meters)

Trail Route	Length of Degraded Trail by Condition Class						Percent
	I	II	III	IV	Others	Total	Degraded
Namche	1,579	797	408	2,702	198	5,684	40.6
Thame	1,009	1,186	34	854	338	3,421	37.2
Kala Patthar I	2,361	1,444	1,674	2,119	541	8,139	45.6
Kala Patthar II	2,236	2,740	1,079	2,466	138	8,659	52.3
Gokyo	3,078	2,993	123	2,605	431	9,230	45.3
Chhukhung	946	0	118	506	68	1,638	36.2
Chola	1,212	811	0	377	239	2,639	39.9
Total	12,421	9,971	3,436	11,629	1,953	39,410	44.2

Source: Nepal (1999), p.219.

Irrespective of the condition class categories, overall, Kala
Patthar II and I are the most affected trails, followed by Gokyo and
Namche. However, if the highest level of degradation (*i.e.*, Class
IV) is considered, Namche tops the list with 19 per cent of its trail
exhibiting such condition, followed by Kala Patthar II (14.9 per
cent), Gokyo (12.8 per cent), Kala Patthar I (11.9 per cent),
Chhukhung (11.1 per cent), Thame (9.3 per cent), and Chola (5.7
per cent). This is understandable because Namche and Everest Base
Camp are the most popular trails in the region. The Namche trail
provides the only access to the Park from outside; only a few visitors come from the westerly direction by crossing the Tashi Lapcha

pass and arrive at Thame. The Everest Base Camp is located at the terminus of Kala Patthar Route II, and is the most popular trekking destination in the Park. Two separate analyses, one conducted with the aid of a geographic information system, and the other applying multivariate statistics, indicated strong correlations between high levels of impacts and vegetation (more impacts in shrub/grassland zone), altitude (more frequency of impacted trails at high altitude), trail grade (high levels of impacts on a grade > 25 per cent), visitor density (more impacts on high traffic routes), and location of tourist facilities (Nepal, 1999). Very little evidence of trail maintenance was found in Khumbu.

DISCUSSION

Tourism-induced environmental changes, as discussed above indicates a gradual transformation of both the natural and cultural landscape of the Everest region. It is true that historically local *Sherpa* have been living in a partly-modified natural landscape (Byers, 1987), however, the processes of modification, which in some cases are undesirable, have been very rapid since the advent of tourism, and especially since the early 1990s. The pre-dominantly rural character of the region has given way to a more urban-like landscape. From the perspective of a regional geography, tourism modified space now consists of four major zones of influence: (i) a core region, primarily dependent on tourism and urban-like built up areas and physical facilities, (ii) an intermediate zone that consists of several tourism nodes (transshipment points for tourists, or points of attractions), where the dependency on tourism is significant but other alternative economic activities (trading and agriculture) are present as well, (iii) a secondary zone where tourism ceases to be important and traditional activities dominate the economy, and (iv) a peripheral zone, where there are no tourist attractions, or have not been developed but the economy is dependent on income from tourism (Figure 4.3). Namche Bazaar and Lukla are located in the core zone. Villages such as Thame and Pheriche are in the intermediate zone, while villages beyond the reach of the majority of tourists are located in the secondary zone. A peripheral zone extends outside the Everest region, encompassing villages at the lower altitudinal belts and neighboring districts. Apart from the four zones, a tourism corridor links major transshipment points to the core zone. Villages along the main trekking corridor between Lukla and Everest Base Camp are in this category, and rely almost entirely on tourism. Thus, tourism-induced environmental changes vary across these different regions; significant impacts have occurred in and around the core zone, and decline in frequency and intensity in peripheral zones.

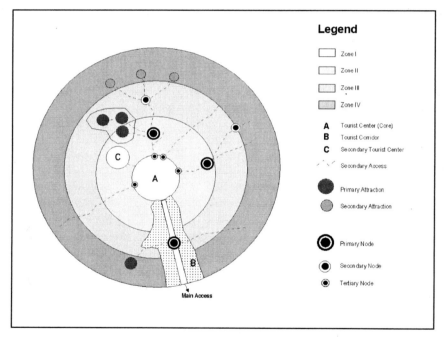

Figure 4.3: Tourism Influence Zones in the Mt. Everest Region.

This chapter presents a cumulative assessment of tourism impacts on the environment of the Mt. Everest region. While there is no question that tourism has provided tremendous economic benefits to the local communities, the environmental costs associated with the development of tourism must not be discounted either. In the absence of a strategic focus on the type and intensity of activities to be promoted, environmental conservation measures to be put in place, and the decisions related to governance, control and regulations, the net positive effects of tourism development in remote mountains such as the Everest region will be very little.

In the developed countries the concern for environmental conservation has led to conflicts between tourism operators and public interest groups. The ski industries in the United States, Canada, Switzerland, and Austria illustrate this problem (Messerli, 1992; Zimmerman, 1992; Goeldner, 1996). Government representatives have begun to take action against some ski resorts that fail to comply with existing environmental laws. Similar actions are needed in the Everest region, particularly against those tourism entrepreneurs who fail to adopt good environmental practices. The problem in the Everest region, however, is the lack of a jurisdictional body that would control and regulate tourism development and enforce regulations regarding good environmental practices. Currently, neither the Park authority nor the tourism ministry has any say on what type of development may be permitted, where, how and by whom. It is entirely up to the independent entrepreneurs to decide on the type, scale, and management practices of their tourism operations. Thus, a local level tourism authority, based on community involvement, should be established to develop and implement such policies, and the authority should be empowered by national legislations. Consistent and long-term policies regarding fuelwood consumption, forest conservation and reforestation, adoption of alternative fuel energy sources, garbage management, trail repairs and restoration, designation of sites for tourist accommodations and other such facilities, development of skilled manpower, and effective visitor education and awareness programs are needed for sustaining tourism in the region.

Several impact mitigation efforts are currently underway, which are mainly supported by various donors, local non-governmental agencies, and the government. These include the establishment of a local Sherpa run NGO, community forestry programs, reforestation, development of hydropower and other alternative energy sources, and solid waste management. While the local community has appreciated these efforts, their desire to sustain these through community participation, local resource mobilization, and developing a sense of ownership of the place and the responsibility to tackle these issues are significantly lacking (Nepal, 2000). Thus, in the absence of a strong local commitment to resolve local problems, outside agencies can only address the symptoms but not the root causes of the problem. The root causes are the lack of a strong coordination between agencies involved in tourism and sustainable development, lack of partnership between the government and local communities, and the absence of appropriate rules and regulations and the means to enforce the regulations.

These and many other issues, such as inequitable access to tourism opportunities, have resulted in a situation, where few influential tourism operators exploit common property resources at the expense of the community. It is perhaps appropriate to state that a small-scale "tragedy of commons" is at work in the Everest region. Tourism has provided the necessary platform for policy-making and the incentives for local communities and organizations to address not only tourism-induced negative environmental impacts but also broader concerns for environmental management and sustainable development. It is now up to the local communities to decide which path they would like to be on: the path towards a short-term boom-and-bust development, or toward a sustained and holistic development based on collective wisdom, sense of ownership and responsibility, and a futuristic vision.

CONCLUSIONS

Tourism in mountainous environments pose specific challenges not encountered elsewhere. Mountain-specific characteristics such as inaccessibility, fragility, diversity, niche, and marginality have significant implications for the type, intensity, and nature of tourism development in the mountains. These characteristics are greatly relevant when discussing the effects of tourism in the Everest region.

Four broad conclusions can be made from this study. First, there is a considerable variation in the type, magnitude, and extent of environmental impacts in the Everest region. Impacts including garbage accumulation and trails tend to concentrate at major tourist centers and along popular trekking routes. Impacts on forests are highly localized, and have not diminished even after the successful introduction of several alternative energy sources. Trail impacts depend on not just the amount of use but are greatly influenced by topographical and locational factors, including altitude, vegetation, trail grade, and cluster of human settlements and tourist facilities. These environmental costs need to be accounted for when considering the net benefits from tourism.

Secondly, the impacts on local forests illustrate the spatial continuities of tourism-induced problems, *i.e.*, events in one area have implications for other areas. For example, the demand for fuelwood in tourist centers such as Namche Bazaar has led to degradation of forests in non-tourist areas, especially outside the Park boundary. This is an unintended consequence of the enforcement rule that the Park authority has imposed on local people, which prohibits them from cutting trees inside the Park boundary. This illustrates the fact that parks should not be considered island entities, and that conservation must take into consideration the interconnectedness between regions. Impacts on local forests are thus a function of resource availability, access, opportunities and management options.

Thirdly, tourism has accelerated the processes of modification of the natural and cultural landscape. In particular, it has changed significantly the size, character, and functions of rural settlements in the region. The presence and the influence of tourism is greatly felt in settlements as remote as the Everest region. As a response to tourism-led development, various zones of influence are now evolving.

Finally, in the context of sustainable tourism in the Everest region, it is relevant to consider Müller's proposition, which states that tourism in the mountains must be characterized by environmental friendliness and efficiency, authenticity, slow development, and management based on a people-centered philosophy (Müller, 1996).

REFERENCES

Bjønness, I. (1980) "Ecological conflicts and economic dependency on tourist trekking in Sagarmatha (Mt. Everest) National Park, Nepal. An alternative approach to park planning," *Norsk Geografisk Tiddskrift*, 34: 119-138.

Blangy, S. and Vautier, S. (2001) "Europe", in Weaver, D.B. (ed.), *The Encyclopedia of Ecotourism*, Oxon, UK: CAB International, 155-171.

Byers, A. (1987) *A Geoecological Study of Landscape Change and Man Accelerated Soil Loss: The Case of Sagarmatha (Mt. Everest) National Park, Khumbu, Nepal*, Ph.D Thesis, Boulder, CO: Department of Geography, University of Colorado.

Byers, A. (2002) *Tourism and Deforestation in the Mt. Everest Region of Nepal*, Unpublished draft, 39 pp.

Canadian Tourism Commission (2003) www.canadatourism.com/ en/ctc/ctx/newsdirect accessed February 14, 2003.

Fennell, D. (2001) "Anglo-America," in Weaver, D.B. (ed.), *The Encyclopedia of Ecotourism*, Oxon, UK: CAB International, 107-122.

Fischbacher, C. (1999) *Entwicklung durch Technik*, Wien: OEFSE, Österreichische Forschungsstiftung für Entwiklungshilfe.

Garratt, K.A.J. (1981) *Sagarmatha National Park Management Plan*, Department of National Parks and Wildlife Conservation, His Majesty's Government, Nepal.

Ghimire, K. (2002) "Regional tourism and South-South economic cooperation," *Geographical Journal*, 167(2): 99-110.

Goeldner, C. (1996) "North American alpine tourism development – competition, obstacles, strategies, consequences," in Weiermair, K. (ed.), *Proceedings - Alpine Tourism, Sustainability: Reconsidered and Redesigned*, Innsbruck: University of Innsbruck, 95-114.

Hardie, N. (1987) *Nepal-New Zealand Project of Forest Management in Khumbu-Pharak*, Unpublished report to the Himalayan Trust and Voluntary Service Abroad.

Ives, J.D. and Messerli, B. (1990) *The Himalayan Dilemma, Reconciling Development and Conservation*, London, UK: The United Nations University.

Jefferies, B.E. (1982) "Sagarmatha National Park: the impact of tourism in the Himalayas", *Ambio*, 11(1): 274-81.

Jefferies, M. (1985) *Sagarmatha Mother of the Universe - The Story of Mt. Everest National Park*, Auckland: Cobb/Horwood Publications.

Lew, A.A. (2001) "Asia", in Weaver, D.B. (ed.), *The Encyclopedia of Ecotourism*, Oxon, UK: CAB International, 123-137.

Mattle, B. (1999) *Räumliche und zeitliche Entwicklung der touristischen Infrastruktur in Khumbu, Nepal*, Diplomarbeit, Philosphisch-naturwissenschaftliche Fakultät, Universität Bern.

Messerli, B. and Ives, J.D. (eds.) (1997) *Mountains of the World: A Global Priority*, New York: Parthenon, Sagarmatha Pollution Control Committee.

Messerli, P. (1992) "Integrated development of tourism - a strategy to cope with environmental and economic uncertainities: experience from the Swiss Alps", in Gill, A. and Hartman, R. (eds.), *Mountain Resort Development: Proceedings of the Vail Conference*, 18-21 April 1991, Burnaby, BC: Centre for Tourism Policy and Research, Simon Fraser University.

Mountain Agenda (1999) *Mountains of the World – Tourism and Mountains*, Berne: Mountain Agenda.

Müller, H. (1996) "Freizeittrends und Freizeitverhalten - Stellenwert des alpinen Bergurlaubs", in Weiermair, K. (ed.), *Proceedings - Alpine Tourism, Sustainability: Reconsidered and Redesigned*, Innsbruck: University of Innsbruck, 176-85.

Nepal, S. (1999) *Tourism Induced Environmental Changes in the Nepalese Himalaya: A Comparative Analysis of the Everest, Annapurna, and Mustang Regions*, Ph.D Thesis submitted to the Faculty of Natural Sciences, Switzerland: University of Berne.

Nepal, S.K. (2000) "Tourism, national parks, and local communities", in Butler, R.W. and Boyd, S. (eds.), *Tourism in National*

Parks – Issues and Implications, Chichester: John Wiley, 73-94.

Nepal, S.K. (2002) "Examining tourism impacts from an interdisciplinary perspective", *Asiatische Studien*, LV 3: 777-804.

Nepal, S.K., Kohler, T. and Banzhaf, B. (2002) *Great Himalaya: Tourism and the dynamics of change in Nepal*, Berne: Swiss Foundation for Alpine Research.

Pawson, I.G., Stanford, D.D., Adams, V.A. and Norbu, M. (1984) "Growth of tourism in Nepal's Everest Region: impact on the physical environment and structure of human settlements", *Mountain Research and Development*, 4(3): 237-46.

Sharma, P. (2000) *Tourism as Development: Case Studies from the Himalaya*, Kathmandu: Himal Books and STUDIEN Verlag.

SPCC (1997) Annual Report for the Fiscal Year 1996-1997, Publisher and place published not specified.

Stevens, S.F. (1993) *Claiming the Highground. Sherpas, Subsistence, and Environmental Change in the Highest Himalaya*, Berkeley: University of California Press.

Stone, P. (ed.) (1992) *The State of the World's Mountains - A Global Report*, New Jersey: Zed Books Ltd.

Williams, P.W., Singh, T.V. and Schlüter, R. (2001) "Mountain ecotourism: Creating a sustainable future", in Weaver, D.B. (ed.), *The Encyclopedia of Ecotourism*, Oxon, UK, CAB International, 205- 218.

World Tourism Organization (1998) WTO News, January/February.

World Travel and Tourism Council (1999) *Travel and Tourism's Economic Impact*, Brussels, Belgium.

Yee, J.G. (1992) *Ecotourism Market Survey: A Survey of North American Tour Operators*, San Francisco: The Intelligence Center, Pacific Asia Travel Association.

Zimmermann, F. (1992) "Issues, problems and future trends in the Austrian Alps: the changes within traditional tourism", in Gill, A. and Hartman, R. (eds.), *Mountain Resort Development: Proceedings of the Vail Conference*, 18-21 April 1991, Burnaby, B.C.: Centre for Tourism Policy and Research, Simon Fraser University, 160-70.

5

Tourism Dynamics in the Urban-Rural Fringe

David Weaver

INTRODUCTION

Within North America, and to a lesser extent other developed regions, the urban-rural fringe or 'exurbs' have emerged as an increasingly dominant expression of the post-modern cultural landscape. I argue in this chapter that the urban-rural fringe is also an increasingly important venue for an array of tourism-related activities, and that the distinctive nature of these activities justifies the articulation of 'exurban tourism' as a distinct topic of investigation within the field of tourism studies. The first section defines and describes the urban-rural fringe, and this is followed by a description of the tourism activities that occur therein, and the extent to which the fringe has been addressed within the tourism literature. Subsequently, the major issues and characteristics that distinguish exurban tourism are discussed, toward making the case for its recognition as a distinctive and significant focus of future tourism research.

URBAN-RURAL FRINGE

In simplest terms, the urban-rural fringe is a transitional zone between spaces that are clearly urban and clearly rural. Daniels (1999) argues that the urban-rural fringe emerged during a third and most recent phase of North American urban expansion that has involved the large-scale movement of urban and suburban residents to rural areas adjacent to the city. This facet of 'counter-urbanization' (Berry and Gillard, 1977) followed earlier mass migrations of rural residents to urban areas, and subsequently of urban (and mainly white) residents to the suburbs. The urban-rural fringe is the product of cumulative decisions by individuals to establish residences and businesses based on compromises between significant 'push' and 'pull' motivations. Many residents are 'pushed' away from the city by perceived problems of congestion, escalating crime, high cost of living, deterioration of infrastructure and services, and in some cases by concern over rapid ethnic change. Concurrently, they are 'pulled' toward the countryside by the prospect of larger and cheaper properties, better prospects for owning rather than renting, lower taxes, greater freedom in the use of land, lower crime, better social interactions, and a cleaner and non-congested physical environment (Bowles and Beesley, 1991; Daniels, 1999; Wolf, 1999).

Surveys consistently reveal that low-density, semi-rural environments are preferred as residential settings by a majority of Americans (Lucy and Phillips, 2000). However, because these migrants still maintain vital connections with the city through employment and the desire to access 'big-city' attractions such as restaurants and theatre, they try to locate as close to the city as possible in order to minimize commuting times and distances. Facilitating the contemporary migration of urbanites into the near countryside are factors such as increased prosperity, the automobile-centric nature of North American culture (which makes private vehicle commuting an acceptable transportation option), and the diffusion of home workplace arrangements that reduce the need for daily commutes. In addition, the emergence of edge cities (concentrations of business and retail activity in the outer suburbs) allows people to reside even farther into the countryside by eliminating the traditional need to commute all the way into the central business district (Garreau, 1991).

The urban-rural fringe essentially evolves, therefore, as the result of trade-offs between the relative advantages of urban and rural location. As described by Davis et al. (1994), exurban residents as a result tend to display hybrid characteristics and behaviour:

> While exurban households derive their incomes from
> urban jobs, their members may consider themselves pri-
> marily farmers purchasing farms of varying sizes to
> effect this desire. They may not feel the need for the
> social services offered in urban areas, but they do not
> wish to be too far away from them. They may want
> small-scale government and basic, low-cost govern-
> ment services such as police, fire protection, and educa-
> tion. They may value accessibility to outdoor recreation
> opportunities more highly than suburban households
> do. They may be very conscious of the environment.
> While rural households depend on resource exploitation
> for a living, exurban households flee the city to enjoy
> unexploited resources. Overall, exurban households
> may be more like rural households in sociocultural
> aspects, but more like urban households in economic
> and environmental aspects. (p. 46)

Similar motivations apply to exurban businesses and industries, which desire proximity to urban markets as well as the cheaper land costs and lower tax advantages that derive from a more rural loca-tion. The latter considerations are especially germane to businesses such as airports, cemeteries, nurseries, raceways and waste dispos-al sites that require a relatively large amount of operational space. When large-lot housing subdivisions, 'farmettes', hobby farms, urban-specialized farms (*e.g.*, horse farms, orchards, market gar-dens), traditional farms, remnant woodlands, retail strips and other typical land uses are juxtaposed with these industries, the urban-rural fringe emerges as an extremely complex amalgam of primary, secondary and tertiary activities distributed among a diversity of residence types.

Various attempts have been made to define the urban-rural fringe, which is also variably known under the terms 'rural-urban fringe', 'fringe', 'metropolitan fringe', 'exurbs', 'exurbia', 'urban hinterland', 'urban field', 'peri-urban', 'urban shadow', 'urban-rural continuum', 'semi-suburbs', 'post-suburbs', 'semi-rural' and 'semi-urban'. These terms all serve to refute the simple urban-rural dichotomy that no longer accurately describes the North American landscape. However, this widespread recognition of transitional dynamics, which commenced in the mid-twentieth century with the work of Spectorsky (1955), does not mean that its contours are well defined.   First, there is the issue of definitional variability. McKenzie (1996) defines the urban-rural fringe as the space between the edge of a city's contiguous development (a structural criterion) and the outer edge of the commuting zone (a functional criterion). In larger cities, this may result in an urban-rural fringe 120 kilometres or more in width (Davis *et al.*, 1994). Others (*e.g.*, Nelson, 1991 and Daniels, 1999) suggest spatial density thresholds (*e.g.*, population density and proportion of open space) and/or polit-ical criteria (*e.g.*, counties or census tracts that comprise a recog-nized metropolitan area). Secondly, even if consensus is reached on a definition, there is the added problem of chronic instability where-in the outer edge of the fringe is continually encroaching on rural space while the urban area is continually encroaching into the near fringe.

These fuzzy and shifting boundaries of exurbia exemplify the post-modern landscape, but render difficult the measurement of its size and population at any given time. Nevertheless, Wolf (1999) estimates that exurban environments account for almost one-third of the land area of the lower 48 states of the US (or about 2.4 mil-lion km^2) and almost one-quarter of its population (or about 60 mil-lion residents). Of particular interest are areas of metropolitan con-vergence such as the Boston-Washington corridor where the exurbs have coalesced into contiguous and extensive fringe-regions. It is further generally averred that the exurbs are the fastest growing type of landscape in North America in population terms, as the continu-al arrival of new migrants and expansion of the outer edge more than compensate for the loss of territory to urban sprawl. The reference to US examples in the above discussion is not accidental, since factors well represented in that country have been particularly amenable to the development of the urban-rural fringe. These include a legacy of relatively relaxed zoning and planning proto- cols, a near-universal fixation with the private vehicle, a cultural preference for single-family dwellings on large lots, and widespread cultural ambivalence toward urban areas that are increasingly seen as dangerous and undesirable. Europe tends more toward the tradi- tional model of the urban-rural dichotomy, while Canada (Beesley, 1991; Beesley and Russwurm, 1981) and Australia (McKenzie, 1997) are somewhere in between but probably closer to the US pat- tern.

TOURISM ACTIVITY IN THE URBAN-RURAL FRINGE

In addition to the land uses outlined above, the urban-rural fringe also typically accommodates a pattern of tourism activity that is dis- tinctively 'exurban' in form and function. The four categories of activity that characterize the exurban tourism sector are theme parks and allied attractions, tourist shopping villages, modified nature- based tourism, and touring. Theme parks and their allies (*e.g.*, wildlife parks, amusement parks) are comparable to airports, ceme- teries and waste disposal sites in that their location is a compromise between access to urban markets and access to large amounts of rel- atively inexpensive rural land. Canadian examples include Canada's Wonderland and the African Lion Safari, both of which occupy sites in the urban-rural fringe of the Greater Toronto Area. In Australia, Dream World, MovieWorld and Wet n'Wild are three theme/amusement parks located in the exurbs of the Gold Coast. Exurban locations also tend to characterize American theme park chains such as Six Flags and Paramount. While many theme parks and amusement parks also occupy resort and non-resort urban loca- tions, some of these (*e.g.*, Disneyland in Anaheim, California) have exurban origins that were subsequently erased by urban expansion (IAAPA, 2002).

Tourist shopping villages (TSVs) are small towns or villages that base their tourism mainly on retail attractions, usually along a business strip (Getz, 1993). The typical TSV possesses a small downtown that once functioned as a true central business district for a surrounding rural area, but has since been wholly or partially converted into a recreational business district dominated by boutiques, restaurants, galleries and other establishments that cater wholly or mainly to a tourist clientele. Canadian exurban examples include St. Jacob's and Elora (in the western portion of the Greater Toronto Area) and Bragg Creek, Okotoks and Cochrane, all near Calgary. Tamborine Mountain is the primary TSV in the urban-rural fringe of the Gold Coast, while the villages of Maleny and Montville jointly serve a similar function in the exurbs of the nearby Sunshine Coast (a major resort area north of Brisbane). TSVs are also found in the urban-rural fringe of most US metropolitan areas, including Washington (*e.g.*, Warrenton and Middleburg). As with theme parks, some TSVs are currently urban but first emerged in an exurban locale (*e.g.*, Occaquan, in the greater Washington metro area). Others are found in rural tourism regions or along major rural transportation arteries.

The third tourism-related activity involves recreational visits to remnant or extensive natural or semi-natural areas. The Niagara Escarpment and Oak Ridges Moraine constitute two such venues in the Greater Toronto Area, while Lamington and Tamborine Mountain National Parks are the most important examples in the Gold Coast region. In most cases, these open spaces are also protected areas (*e.g.*, National Parks, Regional Parks, Conservation Areas) whose mandate includes a greater or lesser tendency to accommodate various recreational activities.

Finally, the urban-rural fringe is an important venue for touring. While much of this activity involves private vehicle-based groups appreciating the semi-rural nature of the landscape, a formal element consisting of regular bus tours and organized circuits is also discernable. Of particular importance is the emergence of wine-based tours and circuits in Canada (*e.g.*, Niagara Peninsula), Australia (*e.g.*, the Hunter Valley of New South Wales and the Barossa Valley of South Australia) and the US (*e.g.*, the Napa and Sonoma Valleys).

ACADEMIC STATUS OF EXURBAN TOURISM

Considerable academic research has been undertaken on the tourism activities described above, and especially with respect to theme parks and TSVs. However, almost no attempts have been made to examine these phenomena within the specific context of the urban-rural fringe, despite the importance of these activities in this area. For example, the literature on theme parks tends to emphasise either the practical business considerations of such facilities (*e.g.*, Braun and Soskin, 1999; Milman, 2001) or their status as a contentious sociological phenomenon (*e.g.*, Sorkin, 1992; Hollinshead, 1998; Warren, 1999). Several studies do consider the factors underlying the decision to locate theme parks within certain areas (*e.g.*, Foglesong, 1999), but even these fail to contextualize their analysis within an exurban dynamic. The literature on TSVs is similarly extensive but bereft. These include studies of St. Jacob's, Acton, Elora and other destinations within the Greater Toronto Area (Dahms, 1991; Getz, 2000; Mitchell and Coghill, 2000), and of TSVs in the greater Calgary area (Getz *et al.*, 1994). A notable exception is Weaver and Lawton (2001), who place their study of resident perceptions in Tamborine Mountain in the context of the urban-rural fringe of Australia's Gold Coast. (Further aspects of this research are detailed in the discussion below.) Studies of tourism in natural or near-natural areas in the fringe can be found in the eco-tourism and outdoor recreation literature, while Hall *et al.* (2000), among others, features wine tourism with an implicit exurban component.

Within the broader tourism literature, the sub-fields of rural tourism (*e.g.*, Page and Getz, 1997; Butler *et al.*, 1997) and urban tourism (*e.g.*, Murphy, 1997; Tyler *et al.*, 1998; Judd and Fainstein, 1999; Bull and Church, 2001) are well established, but no consideration has been given thus far to the possibility of the exurbs as a distinctive focus. But if the tourism literature has neglected the urban-rural fringe, it is also fair to say that the study of the urban-rural fringe within geography and other social sciences has neglected tourism. For example, a major study of the Australian urban-rural fringe (McKenzie, 1996) makes only tangential reference to tourism, as do major Canadian sources such as Beesley and Russwurm (1981) and Beesley (1991). One notable mention is Lamb (1983), who suggests that the farthest limit of an outward recreational excursion can be used to demarcate the outer limit of the urban-rural fringe.

CHARACTERISTICS AND ISSUES: TOWARD A SUB-FIELD OF EXURBAN TOURISM?

The following discussion is intended to initiate debate as to which tourism-related issues are especially relevant in the urban-rural fringe, toward the recognition of this area as a distinct and worthy focus of investigation within tourism studies.

Distinct Product Amalgam

The four types of tourism activity described above together constitute a distinct exurban tourism product. Most germane to this profile is the emergence of these activities as the product of compromise between the advantages of urban and rural location. Relevant topics of investigation include whether tourism in the near-urban fringe (*i.e.*, where considerations of urban advantage prevail) is distinct from tourism in the near-rural fringe, and whether tourism in the urban-rural fringe of large metropolitan areas such as Toronto and Washington is distinct from that found in mid-sized cities such as the Gold Coast or Ottawa. Of potential interest to the development of exurban tourism theory are the diverse origins of these attractions. TSVs are an example of functional adaptation wherein *in situ* cultural resources (*i.e.*, the CBD of a rural service centre) are converted from a traditional tertiary function (supplying basic goods and services to local residents) to a post-modern tertiary function (supplying 'luxury' goods and services to visitors). Functional adaptation in open spaces and woodlands is indicated by the transition from primary exploitation (agriculture and logging) to tertiary recreational uses. Theme parks, in contrast, are specialized built attractions that are imposed on a selected location. While TSVs are amenable to analysis through the resort life cycle model, theme and amusement parks exemplify the 'instant resort' anomaly recognised by Butler (1980).

Both adaptation and imposition are therefore evident in the exurban tourism landscape. However, the spatial and functional relationships among these attractions need to be investigated. Is theme park location influenced by proximity to TSVs, touring circuits and open recreational areas? And to what extent is the rate and form of TSV development in one town or village influenced by proximity to other TSVs? For example, does the conversion of St. Jacobs into a TSV account for the lack of such development in nearby Elmira due to the dynamics of intervening opportunity or other factors? Research is also required to determine whether tourists are likely to 'package' certain attractions in a trip to the fringe. Preliminary evidence is offered by Tamborine Mountain, where a high portion of visitors to the local TSV also cited the local National Park and the trip itself (*i.e.*, the tour) as integral components of the experience (Weaver and Lawton, 2001). In contrast, the all-day nature of the typical theme park visit (induced in part by the desire to obtain maximum returns from a day-long, unlimited use pass) suggests that such facilities may be isolated from the integrated trio of TSV, open space and circuit tour that is suggested by the Tamborine Mountain research. Important marketing and product development implications derive from this proposed pattern.

Distinct Market Profile

At least three notable characteristics appear to characterize the exurban tourist market. First, the line between tourists *per se* and local recreationalists who do not meet applicable 'domestic tourist' criteria is blurred, since both groups are well represented among visitors. Complicating this situation in larger metropolitan areas is the fact that some or all residents of an adjacent urban area may meet the 80-kilometre or 50-mile one-way threshold in the farther reaches of the fringe. The tourist/local dichotomy may be semantic from the practical perspective of product management, but the issue is significant for those who emphasize the importance of distinguishing external revenue inputs (*i.e.*, from 'tourists') from local revenue that is 'merely' redistributed. A similar external/internal dynamic applies to crowding, stress on infrastructure, etc., while local visitors are also often perceived to generate fewer negative cultural or social impacts. Such distinctions are also evident in urban areas, but the fact that both locals and tourists are represented in large proportions suggests that this issue and its implications are particularly important in the urban-rural fringe.

Second, the exurban market is overwhelmingly comprised of day-only visitors (*i.e.*, excursionists) since most visitors maintain overnight accommodations or residences in the adjacent urban area. This, again, is an advantage of urban proximity that can save a large amount on the cost of a visit. However, this results in a skewed tourism system wherein the normally dominant accommodation sector – usually a major generator of destination revenue - is typically represented by just a small number of B&Bs or similar establishments. Third, proximity to urban areas generates an enormous market in both absolute and relative terms, giving rise to exurban 'hyper-destinations' such as Tamborine Mountain, where 7,000 residents accommodate about 500,000 visitor-days per year. Even more impressively, the 1,500 residents of St. Jacobs contend each year with an estimated 1-3 million visitors. Similar levels of visitation apply to larger theme parks, circuit tours and designated open spaces, though these occur beyond the confines of an actual village or town. While the implications of such high levels of visitation are well covered in the literature, some of the characteristics associated with the fringe may exacerbate these impacts, while others may be ameliorative (see below).

Instability

The urban-rural fringe is characterized by rapid population growth and constant landscape change involving a complex array of land uses and activities. The instability that this entails, which has profound implications for tourism, can be illustrated by applying the life cycle concept to the area's pattern of overall development. As depicted in Figure 5.1, a given location in the fringe was once a relatively stable rural area of low population and minimal population growth. This is analogous to the 'exploration' stage of the destination life cycle. The cycle of escalating urban intrusion that marks the area's incorporation into the urban-rural fringe is in turn analogous with the 'involvement', 'development' and 'consolidation' stages of the resort cycle. When the area finally 'fills in' and becomes a stable, highly populated urban area, then something comparable to 'stagnation' is evident. Using this model, the urban-rural fringe can therefore be defined as an area experiencing chronic volatility in its transition from a stable rural to a stable urban space.

If the destination life cycle model is superimposed over this overall development life cycle model, then the exploration stage occurs when the area is still rural. The involvement, development and consolidation stages all occur during the exurban phase of the area, and stagnation sets in once the area is urban. I argue, therefore, that the urban-rural fringe is characterized by the concurrence of the most volatile period of the destination life cycle with the most volatile period of the overall development life cycle. Not surprisingly, this gives rise to a situation of endemic uncertainty and conflict. The urban-rural fringe has been described as an area of collision

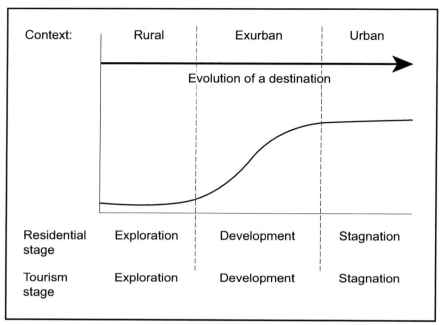

Figure 5.1: Residential and Tourism Life Cycles in the Urban-Rural Fringe.

between city and country (Daniels, 1999), a zone of *competition and conflict* (Troughton, 1981), and an area of urban *invasion* (Walker, 1997). In addition, the term *sprawl* that is generally applied to the exurbs has a strongly negative connotation. Typical foci of conflict in the fringe include competition for the use of scarce resources (*e.g.*, ground water) and inadequate infrastructure (*e.g.*, roads), complaints by residents about farm odours, the juxtaposition of incompatible land uses, and, most tellingly, resentment of the continuing encroachment of new residents and businesses. Thus, any considerations of tourism 'sustainability' in the urban-rural fringe cannot be divorced from the apparent unsustainability of much of what occurs outside of tourism.

To these non-tourism processes and issues may be added in certain locations the rapid growth of the tourism industry, manifested variably by highly congested TSVs, 'instant' theme parks that carve further into the semi-rural landscape, increased crowding of local green space, and the contribution of tour buses and tourists' private vehicles to already congested roads. Unfortunately, and as stated earlier, there have been almost no attempts to investigate the impacts of these tourism activities within the specific context of the urban-rural fringe. One study that may provide some indication of distinctive and complex exurban dynamics is the above-mentioned study of Tamborine Mountain by Weaver and Lawton (2001). This research used hierarchical cluster analysis to stratify local residents into three relatively homogeneous groups, *i.e.*, supporters of tourism (27 per cent), opponents (22 per cent) and a majority of ambivalent neutrals that recognized economic benefits but social and environmental costs (51 per cent). Opposition to tourism was significantly associated with length of residence, with the average 'opponent' residing 12.7 years in the community, compared with 8.7 years for supporters and 9.1 years for neutrals. The opponents, furthermore, were more likely to cite rural-bias factors as the main reason for moving to Tamborine Mountain (*e.g.*, peace and quiet, escape from the city) while supporters were far more likely to cite urban-bias factors such as proximity to work and diverse lifestyles.

This suggests first of all a substantial difference in motivation between long-time residents and more recent arrivals. Viewed through their respective prisms of bias, the long-time residents view tourism as a manifestation of undesirable urban encroachment, while newer residents welcome the diversity of activities that come with tourism, and are happy to share their community with visitors. Newer residents, moreover, moved into Tamborine Mountain at a time when landscape change was already well underway, while long-time residents maintain a more truly rural and more nostalgic local landscape as their frame of reference for comparison. Opponents and long-time residents are also more likely to complain about the influx of new residents, suggesting a link between their feelings about tourism and about development intensification more generally in the urban-rural fringe. Ironically, it is likely that almost all migrants to Tamborine Mountain found out about the location as tourists – long-time residents as 'explorers' during the rural phase, and new residents as 'mass tourists' during the development stage.

Tamborine Mountain residents are strongly united in their desire to maintain the unique identity of their town, with 90 per cent strongly agreeing or agreeing that the latter is a unique destination that should not imitate the Gold Coast. This implies resistance to the assimilation of Tamborine Mountain into the contiguous urban mass of its dominant beach resort neighbour. However, as revealed above, residents are seriously divided in their views toward tourism, with two-thirds agreeing or strongly agreeing that tourism has divided the community. This is not an unexpected finding given the endemic conflict that characterizes the urban-rural fringe. A similar portion of residents also agrees or strongly agrees that tourism in their community is not being properly planned and managed. This aligns with the assertion of Daniels (1999) and others that the fringe (particularly in the US context) is a bastion of laissez-faire capitalist dynamics as well as lax and fragmented planning protocols. Political fragmentation and other factors also mean that the exurban orbit of a given city cannot easily establish a coherent destination identity for itself that will attract tourists and serve as a focal point for coherent regional planning. One important implication is the particular difficulty that might be encountered in any attempt to truncate the development stage of the exurban destination life cycle through the imposition of planning regulations and despite the increasing popularity of alternative capacity-reducing measures such as the use of municipal tax revenue to obtain conservation easements or purchase and preserve open land adjacent to the city (Howe *et al.*, 1997).

CONCLUSION
The discussion above describes some of the diverse dynamics that potentially demarcate the urban-rural fringe as a distinct tourism environment. While attempts have also been made to identify con-

nections and relationships among these dynamics, much more analysis is necessary to establish the credentials of exurban tourism as a worthy focus and distinct sub-field of investigation within the broader community of tourism researchers. This goal may be potentially attainable by working toward an exurban version of the destination life cycle model. Intriguing deviations from the normative model, such as the association of the exurbs with development-stage dynamics, have already been suggested. More broadly, the pervasiveness of instability, fuzzy boundaries, and conflict/competition position the urban-rural fringe as perhaps the ideal venue for appreciating the contours of post-modern tourism dynamics that require unconventional and non-traditional management and planning approaches. If so, then the theoretical and practical outcomes that emerge from the study of tourism in the urban-rural fringe will have important implications for our emerging post-modern society more generally.

REFERENCES

Beesley, K. (ed.) (1991) *Rural and Urban Fringe Studies in Canada*, Toronto: York University/Atkinson College Geographical Monograph No. 21.

Beesley, K. and Russwurm, L. (eds.) (1981) *The Rural-Urban Fringe: Canadian Perspectives*, Toronto: York University/Atkinson College Geographical Monograph No. 10.

Berry, B.J.L. and Gillard, Q. (1977) *Changing Shape of Metropolitan America: Commuting Patterns, Urban Fields, and Decentralization Processes, 1960-1970*, Cambridge, MA: Ballinger.

Bowles, R. and Beesley, K. (1991) "Quality of life, migration to the countryside and rural community growth", in Beesley, K. (ed.), *Rural and Urban Fringe Studies in Canada*, Toronto: York University/Atkinson College Geographical Monograph No. 21,

45-66.

Braun, B. and Soskin, M. (1999) "Theme park competitive strategies", *Annals of Tourism Research*, 26(2): 438-42.

Bull, P. and Church, A. (2001) "Understanding urban tourism: London in the early 1990s", *International Journal of Tourism Research*, 3(2): 141-50.

Butler, R. (1980) "The concept of a tourist area cycle of evolution: implications for management of resources", *Canadian Geographer*, 24: 5-12.

Butler, R., Hall, C. and Jenkins, J. (eds.) (1997) *Tourism and Recreation in Rural Areas*, New York: Wiley.

Dahms, F. (1991) "St Jacobs, Ontario: from declining village to thriving tourist community", *Ontario Geography*, 36: 1-13.

Daniels, T. (1999) *When City and Country Collide: Managing Growth in the Metropolitan Fringe, Washington*, DC: Island Press.

Davis, J., Nelson, A. and Dueker, K. (1994) "The new 'burbs': the exurbs and their implications for planning policy", *Journal of the American Planning Association*, 60(Winter): 45-59.

Foglesong, R. (1999) "Walt Disney World and Orlando: Deregulation as a strategy for tourism", in Judd, D. and Fainstein, J. (eds.), *The Tourist City*, New Haven: Yale University Press, 89-106.

Garreau, J. (1991) *Edge City: Life on the New Frontier*, New York: Doubleday.

Getz, D. (1993) "Tourist shopping villages: development and planning strategies", *Tourism Management*, 14(1): 15-26.

_____ (2000) "Tourist shopping villages: development and planning strategies", in Ryan, C. and Page, S. (eds.), *Tourism Management: Towards the New Millennium*, New York: Pergamon, 211-25.

Getz, D., Joncas, D. and Kelly, M. (1994) "Tourist shopping villages in the Calgary region", *Journal of Tourism Studies*, 5 (1): 2-15.

Hall, C., Sharples, L., Cambourne, B. and Macionis, N. (eds.) (2000) *Wine Tourism Around the World: Development, Management and Markets*, Oxford: Butterworth-Heinemann.

Hollinshead, K. (1998) "Disney and commodity aesthetics: a critique of Fjellman's analysis of 'distory' and the 'historicide' of the past", *Current Issues in Tourism*, 1(1): 58-119.

Howe, J., McMahon, E. and Propst, L. (1997) *Balancing Nature and Commerce in Gateway Communities*, Washington, DC: Island Press.

IAAPA (International Association of Amusement Parks and Attractions) (2002) Facts and Fun: Amusement Facilities Links, http://www.iaapa.org/facts/f-linksa.cfm. (visited 2 September 2002).

Judd, D. and Fainstein, S. (eds.) (1999) *The Tourist City*, New Haven, CT: Yale University Press.

Lamb, R. (1983) "The extent and form of exurban sprawl", *Growth and Change*, 14(1): 40-47.

Lucy, W., and Phillips, D. (2000) *Confronting Suburban Decline: Strategic Planning for Metropolitan Renewal*, Washington, DC: Island Press.

McKenzie, F. (1996) *Beyond the Suburbs: Population Change in the Major Exurban Regions of Australia*, Canberra: Department of Immigration and Multicultural Affairs.

McKenzie, F. (1997) "Growth management or encouragement? A critical review of land use policies affecting Australia's major exurban regions", *Urban Policy and Research*, 15(2): 83-101.

Milman, A. (2001) "The future of the theme park and attraction industry: a management perspective", *Journal of Travel Research*, 40(2): 139-47.

Mitchell, C. and Coghill, C. (2000) "The creation of a cultural heritage landscape: Elora, Ontario, Canada", *Great Lakes Geographer*, 7(2): 88-105.

Murphy, P. (ed.) (1997) *Quality Management in Urban Tourism*, New York: Wiley.

Nelson, A. (1991) "Toward a definition of exurbia", *Journal of Planning Literature*, 6(4): 350-68.

Page, S. and Getz, D. (eds.) (1997) *The Business of Rural Tourism: International Perspectives*, London: International Thomson Business Press.

Sorkin, M. (ed.) (1992) *Variations on a Theme Park*, New York: Hill and Wang.

Spectorsky, A. (1955) *The Exurbanites*, Philadelphia: Lippincott.

Troughton, M. (1981) "The rural-urban fringe: a challenge to resource management", in Beesley, K. and Russwurm, L. (eds.), *The Rural-Urban Fringe: Canadian Perspectives*, Toronto: York University/Atkinson College Geographical Monographs No. 10, 218-43.

Tyler, D., Guerrier, Y. and Robertson, M. (eds.) (1998) *Managing Tourism in Cities: Policy, Process and Practice*, New York: Wiley.

Walker, G. (1997) *An Invaded Countryside: Structures of Life on the Toronto Fringe*, Toronto: York University/Atkinson College Geographical Monographs No. 17.

Warren, S. (1999) "Cultural contestation at Disneyland Paris", in Crouch, D. (ed.), *Leisure/Tourism Geographies: Practices and Geographic Knowledge*, London: Routledge, 109-25.

Weaver, D. (2005) "Residential and Tourism Life Cycles in the Urban-Rural Fringe", *International Journal of Tourism Research*, 7:23-33.

Weaver, D. and Lawton, L. (2001) "Resident perceptions in the urban-rural fringe", *Annals of Tourism Research*, 28(2): 439-58.

Wolf, P. (1999) *Hot Towns: The Future of the Fastest Growing Communities in America*, New Brunswick, NJ: Rutgers University Press.

6

From Heritage to Tourism: A Personal Odyssey

John Tunbridge

All too rarely in academic life, a sublime moment comes along. Someone allows you - even requests you - to reflect aloud on the path you have trodden for forty years and more, the chance patterns, people and places which have guided each turn of the way, and what in essence has brought you from there to here. Such an opportunity to retrace one's steps - and critical path specifically - is more than a privileged self-indulgence, however, it is a source of light cast upon the path ahead. But more importantly, for my audience it may be a source of insight - however individual and idiosyncratic - on the chance steps, and perhaps the missteps, of academic life in general and in particular the shaping of a career in heritage tourism.

I was tempted to subtitle this presentation 'a personal odyssey, or how I fell into bad company'; but second thoughts and conciseness prevailed! Truth to tell, whom you meet and in what context plays a decisive part in the direction you take, and one over which you have little control: you can certainly aim to work with so-and-so, but whether the connection is made, how the chemistry works and what further contacts may develop is not yours to foretell. But in any case there is a good deal more to the story of which the salient points may, I hope, give food for thought.

I persist in the belief that geographers are born, not made. Certainly I was, and I put my vocation to work as a proto-tourist as soon as I could walk. Britain fifty years ago was a fertile place to develop a larger place-awareness. Its first stirrings of affluence were marked by plastic flags which you would stick in the windows of your parents' car to advertise proudly all the places you had 'collected' - even if quantity counted for more than historic quality, of which the advertising thus achieved was rather rudimentary! Independent student wanderings from Cambridge forty years ago allowed the historical dimension of tourism to percolate into one's psyche, particularly when the realization dawned that your point of origin was itself one of the greatest tourist 'honey-pots'. But those were days when student grants covered your university expenses and thereby made your own formative tourism easier than it is for many of my students now.

It was my good fortune to be able to translate those student wanderings into the role of historical-tourism courier/guide to British school parties travelling to continental Europe. This I did for my old high-school geography mentor who directed the travel organization concerned. In following his meticulous itineraries as best I could - and acquiring a profound debt of gratitude in the process - I unwittingly absorbed two critical insights into tourism, specifically what we would now call heritage tourism.

The first was **tourism as a collection of marked sites**: for all destinations there were lists of things to see, and it quickly became apparant that one had to 'collect' them or prove a failure - in one's party's eyes and in one's own! An unspoken 'must see or bust' philosophy prevailed, and it appeared unseemly to ask why: at the Bruges 'Tourist-Historic City' conference in 2002 which led to this presentation, I remained as mystified as I had been thirty-five years before as to why I should 'collect' the Minnewater (charming as it is)! Only through the ensuing years did I learn that, in fact, the most earnest collection list was ultimately doomed to failure. Even if you completed it, there was always someone (in your party if you were unlucky) who would say 'ah, but have you seen...?

The second was **tourism as a syndrome of constraints**. Cost, time, space and information constitute a set of mutually dependent variables that enmesh the tourist in a perennial multidimensional spider's web of constraints, whether or not he/she clearly realizes it - and most of us do not during the romantic dreaming that precedes our travels and, with luck, in selective memories that follow them. Thus are we lulled into yet another round of entanglement. Where tour parties are concerned, there should be some offsetting benefits; but unanticipated constraints tend to multiply geometrically with the numbers in the party, for all are vulnerable to the weakest link, be that health problems, toilet needs or simple impunctuality - as anyone who has ever led a tour group knows all too well. Half a life-time has not erased the memory of trying to get a tour-bus to Prague on time when certain of its occupants had drunk too much good German coffee en route.

These characteristics of tourism have profound implications for the behaviour of tourists in space. While some certainly pioneer new niche interests, or established interests in new locations, tourists en masse gravitate disproportionately to key clusters of sites at the expense of worthy outlying attractions, creating compelling management problems for cities such as Florence or Venice. The geographical models of the 'tourist-historic city' were instantly relatable to these formative insights, when they entered my life twenty years later.

Before this connection was made, I found myself an urban geographer in Canada by 1970, just at the moment when urban geography was both rapidly proliferating and rediscovering its qualitative mission, after the decade-long hegemony of the quantitative revolution. More specifically, here was I in a Canada both in search of its own urban geography and newly aware - especially after the Centennial of Confederation - that it might have a history after all, a history largely visible in its urban places, and a history which arguably defined a distinct national 'heritage' identity at that. For a geographer with a personal background in historically-oriented tourism, it was a short step to both engagement with the concept of heritage and realization of its relevance to emerging Canadian urban geography. If we were moving from urban redevelopment towards greater emphasis upon rehabilitation of existing structures, if we were preserving some as historical icons worthy of pilgrimage, if we were seeking selective conservation of entire city areas, what did this mean for the form, functional and human qualities of our cities - not to speak of their overall image and its marketability? Clearly, I argued, a very great deal.

As the notion and academic discussion of 'heritage' matured it became increasingly apparent to many of us that it was not to be equated with 'history': rather it was a contemporary product, notably reflecting the mindset of what was later conceptualized as a 'postmodern' age, derived from selective exploitation of historical resources. Heritage is the product of particularistic visions, unwittingly partial or deliberately manipulated: herein lies much of its exasperating elusiveness and evanescence, and the compelling need to examine it as a key economic, social and political instrument of our time. It should however be noted that not all who are writing useful things about heritage espouse this view: in recent papers in the Canadian Geographer, Summerby-Murray (2002) clearly does so while Mitchell et al. (2001) imply a more straightforward equation with history.

While the 1970s were the decade of academic engagement with heritage, the 1980s were the decade of critical synergies linking heritage, tourism and cognate issues - for me and for others with whom I found myself on a converging course. Relating how those critical synergies emerged in my own particular circumstances of people, place and intellectual connection, raises the intriguing question of what personal circumstances caused others to converge with me. This is, of course, a more general fascination of the academic vocation; but in our field convergence is, I would judge, a particularly sensitive barometer of the temper of the times.

For me, a critical connection was created by exchange teaching in 1979 at what is now Portsmouth University in England - ironically three years delayed, a tribulation at the time but serendipity in hindsight. There I found myself cross-fertilizing ideas with Gregory Ashworth, just in time before he moved to Groningen. A similar exchange to Pietermaritzburg, South Africa in 1982 produced my first essay on heritage selectivity (Tunbridge, 1984), which rekindled the Ashworth-Tunbridge connection. This essay, simultaneous work on the Byward Market (a heritage focus of Ottawa) and on international waterfront revitalisation, together with those youthful insights, put me in a peculiarly advantageous position both to critique and to globalize Ashworth and de Haan's (1985) early ideas on the 'tourist-historic city'.

So it came to pass that, after a visiting nudge from publisher Iain Stevenson, I found myself signing a contract to co-author the book so titled (Ashworth and Tunbridge, 1990); I vividly recall the trepidation of that moment, on a June day in 1987. What emerged by Christmas 1989 was very much a valedictory of those intellectual convergences of the 1980s; and it fell into place just as the fall of the Berlin Wall was symbolising the dawn of a new era, portending great promise for the further development of heritage tourism and thus for the further articulation of our ideas.

The opening of the formerly socialist world to mass tourism's 'golden horde' in 1990 - and subsequently of other countries formerly subject to Cold War-related constraints, such as South Africa - fuelled an upward trajectory of cognate work through the ensuing decade. With Ashworth and others whose paths intersected, I found myself embroiled in a momentum of mutually reinforcing papers and publications, of which Tunbridge and Ashworth (1996), Graham *et al.* (2000) and Ashworth and Tunbridge (2000) are the most visible products. In the process, long familiar places of academic inspiration were joined by others formerly unknown. So it was that Weimar in eastern Germany, one of the new meccas of heritage tourism, became a 'place icon' of the 1990s in both my research and my enduring affection.

However an interesting reflection on this heritage/tourism related momentum, continuous from 'THC' and seeded much earlier, is that it did not result from a planned agenda, less still from the formally structured research-grant/graduate-student model which is the widely assumed research process today. It resulted from synergies of circumstance and reactive response to requests and opportunities, in which the chance interplay of people and place and the ideas thus engendered have been critical.

In this forum we speak of heritage for tourism, and it is easy to forget that heritage has social and political uses as well as its economic commodification primarily for tourism. But the view from Ottawa is a constant reminder that these other uses may be far more critical, particularly in the bonding of political identities and inculcation of their dominant ideologies. Living in Ottawa has certainly influenced my own appreciation of heritage as an issue much larger than its tourism dimension. The National Capital Commission has a statutory mandate to create a capital for Canadians; its commitment to tourism is essential therefore, to Canadian tourists. This involves not only beautification and promotion of national archival resources (with various other federal agencies), but the conservation and ongoing creation of a built environment reflecting the heritage of all Canadians. Considering what a polyglot bunch we are, that is a very tall order - and it involves selective and creative interpretations which need to evolve through time, as our perception of our collective identity evolves. When I first came, the imperative was to recast a recently British-imperial 'Westminster of the wilderness' into a more recognizably Anglo-French identity; the NCC's Centennial restoration of Sussex Drive in largely francophone Lower Town was a major heritage initiative which, inter alia, supported this goal (Taylor, 1986). Subsequently the multicultural and otherwise multilateral imperative has become dominant. In addition to its collaboration with such expressly multicultural agencies as the Canadian Museum of Civilisation, the NCC has worked to modify the streetscape iconography accordingly, in the core space that it controls. Since it cannot erect monuments to every cultural and otherwise sectional group in this country, it has chosen to foster 'minimalist' heritage expressions of values to which all Canadians might hopefully subscribe: hence the Peacekeeping Monument and the Human Rights Tribute (Tunbridge and Ashworth, 1996). It has, however, increased the specific visibility of groups making a particular claim to monumental representation, hence several women's monuments and the Aboriginal War Memorial. These important statements of social and political identity undoubtedly contribute to heritage tourism interest, at least for those who can read the national code; they have confused at least one foreign tourist, however, Ashworth being under the delusion that the Dutch owned UN peacekeeping!

Tunbridge's personal heritage odyssey does not, therefore, lead to tourism alone, notwithstanding the undoubted importance of tourism in the financing of heritage conservation (Heritage Canada Foundation, 2002). But where does it lead from here? The 'tourist-historic city' certainly remains an evolving idea, as Ashworth eloquently discussed in the conference of that name in Bruges, 2002, from which the invitation to make this presentation emanated. Growing emphasis is being placed upon the 'high culture' component associated with heritage tourism, as was evident in Bruges (see also Evans, 2001). While this may accentuate the crowning achievements of long-established cultural identities, it appears to us that the growing multicultural character of so many tourist-historic cities is a more critical defining element of their future. Social and political harmony might well dictate recognition of the heritage contributions of minorities, including those of recent provenance; this is widely recognized in Canada, as the above discussion implies. But there are fundamental economic and management incentives for tourist-historic cities to co-opt minorities. Products are required to diversify what is on offer, participation in the tourism economy should be broadened, and pressure on existing attraction clusters often needs to be relieved. The growing multicultural orientation - or lack of it - in tourist-historic cities therefore challenges our ongoing study.

There are tangents to every academic field, however, and one particular issue tangential to the tourist-historic city has risen to prominence since the end of the Cold War, abandoned military bases and their adaptive reuse and heritage significance. Waterfront revitalisation is well established in urban heritage tourism, and a growing body of literature has examined former naval bases as exceptional heritage resources within it (Pinder and Smith, 1999). Related to cities, heritage and tourism, if more tenuously, is the recent 'Peace Dividend' closure of many Second World War bases and the frequently pressing question of their adaptive reuse to meet contemporary land use and employment needs. Canada has experienced many US and Canadian forces base closures; it is in the forefront of the issue but it is far from alone. My own long-term attention is focused upon a particular set of bases stretching from Newfoundland (notably Argentia) through Bermuda and the Caribbean to Guyana in former British colonies: they were leased to the US in the famous 'Destroyers for Bases' deal between Churchill and Roosevelt in 1940. As such they possess profound significance as global heritage but a more equivocal significance as local heritage, for the many postcolonial jurisdictions in which they now lie, and a questionable tourism potential in view of perceived recency, utilitarian quality and sometimes environmental despoilation of their material remains. I am hoisting my colours over this particular, tenuous intersection of heritage tourism with post-Cold War base reuse and postcolonialism. Without doubt there are many other borderlands of heritage tourism awaiting intellectual connection with other fields of study. See for example the discussion of rural land conversion from 'productivist' agricultural to amenity/environmental and implicitly heritage-tourism uses in Holmes (2002).

What concluding reflections on heritage tourism can I offer you from the idiosyncrasies of my own experience? At the risk of redundancy, it seems to me that the symbioses and, paradoxically, the tensions between heritage and tourism are inescapable. Leaving aside the heritage borderlands just discussed, tourism is generally pervasive - more or less, sooner or later - and sometimes invasive in heritage issues. Whatever is conspicuously marked as heritage, even if for reasons other than economic, is likely to attract tourism both at the behest of the buyer in quest of new experiences and the seller in quest of means of its support. But this symbiosis is paradoxically also the occasion for tension: those who provide the heritage community's livelihood also peer through its windows and steal its parking spots - ask the citizens of Niagara-on-the-Lake (Mitchell *et al.*, 2001). A further symbiosis/tension is all our very own as academics, the role of the heritage researcher/ field party as tourist(s). We may not care to acknowledge it, but our field pursuit of heritage makes us tourists in the eyes of those with whom we deal - warts and all!

What if any moral is there in the foregoing tale? It certainly is not claimed as the model of how to pursue research. It does however reflect the beauty of academic freedom: the serendipity of happenstance which can flow without a preconceived plan. Were I to start again, I confess I would be a little less inclined to trust to chance and a little more proactive in seeking out opportunity; but, this said, the freedom to adjust one's path to what fortune sends along remains - so far - a priceless gift of academic life, in our field as in others. 'Quo lux ducit' (where light leads), a Latin motto from my academic past, rings in my ears as I write these words.

The academic horizon is not free of clouds, however. Massey (2002) has lamented the contemporary challenge to 'time to think', which threatens free enquiry and considered response to opportunity. It is difficult for me to advise younger academics on how to deal with this, since at my career stage one can often disregard memos and certainly resist the growing pressure to chase research funding. But I've had my share of time stress, and my way of dealing with it is surely timeless. For nearly a dozen years the path of research insight and decision - for this article not least - has been nurtured on the woodland paths of Ottawa's Green Belt, in moments of ostensible truancy, in the company of a now very old dog. His precious gift has been to cut through the 'noise' of life and work, to reach what really matters. He and his predecessor have been comrades through the entire span of my contribution to heritage tourism: whatever value it may have is very much their legacy.

ACKNOWLEDGEMENTS

To a lifetime of mentors and colleagues from my teacher/travel director Max Seidmann to my canine comrade Chimo - and to Elaine who keeps him and me soldiering on.

REFERENCES

Ashworth, G.J. and de Haan, T.Z. (1985) *The Tourist-Historic City: A Model and Initial Application in Norwich, U.K.*, Field Studies Series 6, Groningen: GIRUG.

Ashworth, G.J. and Tunbridge, J.E. (1990) *The Tourist-Historic City*, London: Belhaven.

_____ (2000) *The Tourist-Historic City: Retrospect and Prospect of Managing the Heritage City*, Oxford: Elsevier.

Evans, G. (2001) *Cultural Planning: Towards an Urban Renaissance*, London: Routledge.

Graham, B., Ashworth, G.J. and Tunbridge, J.E. (2000) *A Geography of Heritage: Power, Culture and Economy*, London: Arnold.

Heritage Canada Foundation (2002) *Built Heritage: Assessing a Tourism Resource,* (Research Report), Ottawa: Heritage Canada Foundation.

Holmes, J. (2002) "Diversity and change in Australia's rangelands: a post-productivist transition with a difference?", *Transactions of the Institute of British Geographers,* NS 27(3): 362-384.

Massey, D. (2002) "Time to think", *Transactions of the Institute of British Geographers,* NS27(3): 259-261.

Mitchell, C.J.A., Atkinson, R.G. and Clark, A. (2001) "The creative destruction of Niagara-on-the-Lake", *The Canadian Geographer,* 45(2): 285-299.

Pinder, D. and Smith, H. (1999) "Heritage and change on the naval waterfront: opportunity and challenge", *Ocean and Coastal Management,* 42: 861-889.

Summerby-Murray, R. (2002) "Interpreting deindustrialised landscapes of Atlantic Canada: memory and industrial heritage in Sackville, New Brunswick", *The Canadian Geographer,* 46 (1): 48-62.

Taylor, J.H. (1986) *Ottawa: An Illustrated History,* Toronto: James Lorimer/Canadian Museum of Civilization.

Tunbridge, J.E. (1984) "Whose heritage to conserve? Cross-cultural reflections on political dominance and urban heritage conservation", *The Canadian Geographer,* 28(2): 171-180.

Tunbridge, J.E. and Ashworth, G.J. (1996) *Dissonant Heritage: The Management of the Past as a Resource in Conflict,* Chichester: Wiley.

7

Heritage, Tourism, Quality of Life: "Constructing" New Urban Places

Brian S. Osborne

WHAT'S THE PROBLEM?

The challenges of a post-industrial world are prompting many cities to seek a formula for maintaining economically viable and livable environments. It's an old problem, but it's being acted out in a new context: the loss of former economic functions; decreasing tax-bases; ageing infrastructures; escalating demands for social services. For many cities, therefore, and especially "Historic Cities," marketing heritage, culture, and popular entertainments appears to be the "silver bullet" that alleviates, if not eliminates, these problems.[1]

And there seems to be a demand for it. Established values and traditional practices are being challenged by globalization in economics and communications, diasporic movements of people, and the erosion of traditional values by a pervasive cosmopolitanism that is represented by some as *Westernization*, and by others as *Americanization*. Thus, "heritage" might be another form of "nostalgia" in reaction to a growing sense of anomie as our lives and places lose their distinctiveness in a world of globalized morphings into predictable sameness.

It is this combination of the need for new economic initiatives, nostalgia for an imagined past, and a growing demand for the consumption of entertainment that has made the engagement with the past the stuff of both economic and cultural policy (Osborne, 2002: 16-18). It is all about "place marketing in placeless times" (Robins, 1991). Thus, some places have constructed a tourist industry out of well-established "attraction factors" that have served the tourist-industry well over the last century or more (Jansen-Verbeke, 1985; 1986; 1990; 1991) historical townscapes; aesthetics and cultural performance; marketing the picturesque and the "Other"; consuming the ambience of place. Where these are lacking, other cities-regions have had to "construct" their attractions. Just as nationalizing-states have "invented traditions" (Hobsbawm and Ranger, 1983), so some prospective tourist-cities have had to invent heritage or "storied places": theme parks, ghost tours, romanticized murals, and "historical" re-enactments and displays have all been developed to sell places. In this "making and remaking of place," history and place, heritage and culture, are looked upon as primary resources that can be processed into commodities for sale in an international market (Urry, 1995; Tunbridge and Ashworth, 1996; Ashworth and Howard, 1999; Graham *et al.*, 2000).

But the face of global tourism is changing. The diagnostics of the "Grand Tour" were elitism and limited numbers, that of the mass middle-class tourism of the late-nineteenth century were emerging new travel patterns and bourgeois expectations, while that of the post World War II era was a mass global-tourism associated with ease of travel and a sophisticated infrastructure of accommodations and service provision. But this may be coming to an end. The opening of the twenty-first century is witnessing the emergence of new public expectations in the realms of ecology, heritage, entertainment, and fantasy. And there are new concerns in an age of terrorism, globally transmitted disease, and issues of tourist security in many destinations. The possible onset of a new stage of "Late-Tourism" might require new economic rationales and marketing strategies, will prompt new opportunities and pathologies, and foster distinctive landscapes and communities.

THE SENSE AND "CENTS" OF PLACE?

The economic implications of "place-marketing" are clear. The direct economic impact of tourism is measured in terms of jobs, business profits, and investment in infrastructure. Where the focus is on heritage-tourism and cultural-tourism, a supplementary spin-off is that apart from attracting visitors, the community enhances the amenities and ambience for residents and, thus, attracts new residents and even location-elastic enterprises. Not surprisingly, therefore, many communities in the twenty-first century are evaluating their tourism and heritage potential as they seek economic strategies to replace former industries and commercial activities disrupted by global economic restructuring.

Aware that they are functioning in a world-wide market, tourist-cities have to be competitive in their commodification of distinctive cultural experiences. Several assumptions may be identified. An "escape to reality" through passive or didactic tourism. An "escape to fantasy" for those satiated by facts and who seek "staged authenticity," fantasy, or the hyper-real of Baudrillard's simulacrum (Urry, 1995:140; Baudrillard, 1983:13; Osborne, 2002: 17-18).

But whatever the marketing-strategy, historical-tourist cities are faced with a constant conundrum: the development of a vibrant economic initiative that does not debase the distinctiveness of the place that is being marketed (Ashworth, 2001). Indeed, "sustainability" is at the core of the definition of a viable tourism strategy. Often, this is articulated and comprehended in the context of the ecological and the economic: the prevention of the degrading of the ecosystem or the destruction of the resource-base. But the nurturing of human Quality of Life is at the core of sustainability. Consider the classic definition of sustainable-development in Bruntland's *Our Common Future*:

> ...a process of change in which the exploitation of resources, the direction of investments, the orientation of technological development, and institutional change are all in harmony and enhance both the current future potentials to meet human needs and aspirations

(Bruntland, 1987: 46).

Thus, the balance between growth and sustainability is a crucial issue that must be addressed in terms of each city's unique assemblage of factors of ecology, scale, and social milieu (Hinch, 1996; Faulkner and Tideswell, 1997; Clarke, 1997; Bramwell and Lane, 1999, 2002; Sharpley, 2000; Hardy and Beetob, 2001).[2]

Current tourism strategies may be positioned in the context of four powerful discourses: economic growth; globalization; quality of life; post-tourism.

Bigger is Better, or More is Less?

The *fundamental assumption of the proved-and-tested "Accumulation Model"* of economic growth cannot be contested: cities are economic entities; they have costs; costs have to be covered by tax revenues; the yields of tax revenues depend upon a viable urban-economy; this economy employs resident-workers who also contribute to the municipal tax-base; employed persons contribute to the local consumer economy. From this perspective, heritage-tourism is another economic opportunity with all the intrinsic benefits of investment, employment, and consumption of services. As in the traditional economic growth model, each new tourist enterprise produces a primary economic input and a secondary set of multiplier effects. Growth, therefore, generates increased investments, employment, and revenues in the short term.

However, growth may be attended by indicators of negative feed-back. Thus, the *simple assumptions of* simple growth-stimulation are being challenged by enquiries that privilege the analysis of the impact of increased numbers on facilities, infrastructure, visitor-experience, and the lived-in environment of permanent residents. They question the degree to which revenue-generation derived from transients benefits external investors rather than the local community (Maclaren, 1996; Donald, 2001).

Thus, building on the seminal work of Butler (in Cooper, 1994; Mitchell *et al.*, 2001; Mitchell, 1998) have demonstrated how overly successful tourist-growth is destructive both of the Quality of Life of lived-in places and, ultimately, of the attraction-resource base itself. The basic thesis is that "creative destruction" occurs where unchecked, excessive investment ultimately leads to the erosion of the tourist-attraction for visitor and resident alike by the actions of profit-driven entrepreneurs, cycle of capital accumulation, and the commodification of heritage and distinctive place. Further, the creation of new rational landscapes often destroys the preceding informal ones that constituted the original attraction.

The Mitchell model posits five stages from the initial low-intensity investment in heritage venues, through a stage of more intensive packaging and advertising, followed by increased employment in the heritage-industry and attendant growth of visitor-rates, that, in turn, alienate local residents because of "disintegration of the sense of community and cohesion," and culminates in out-migration, alienation and discontent, and decrease in tourist visits. As Mitchell puts it:

> As a community progresses through these stages, increases occur in investment levels, visitor numbers and negative attitudes towards tourism. This evolution is often inevitable, for in a society driven to accumulate capital, limiting investment is "counter intuitive to the entrepreneurial mind-set" (Mitchell *et al.*, 2001:287).

Further, others are disputing the putative benefits of tourist-growth models as development strategies and arguing that the economic benefits for the host-community are illusory. In this vein, Palmer has challenged the general assumptions of the economic benefits of "cultural businesses" for communities (2002). He argues that the economic benefits are small and Keynesian multiplier effects weak: much of the income generated is taxed away by higher-level government; new income is spent on purchase of goods and services outside the region; employment is low paying, seasonal, and unskilled. For sure, there are beneficiary factors other than economics alone, improved ambience, civic pride, and enhanced community attractiveness. And these may have second-order economic effects.

However, the crucial test of the contribution of simple-growth models of tourist development to the local economy is the impact on the community. Does the community benefit economically or are the proceeds transferred to outside investors? Is the scale of the activity appropriate for the size of the community? Are the range of tourist activities compatible with the ambience of the place? How does the new initiative impact on the Quality of Life of the host community? Clearly, the standard indicators of flows of visitors, revenues generated, and numbers employed are not the only criteria.

The essential argument is that exponential growth in a finite resource base or restricted space is ecologically wrong, socially futile, and generally irrational. For Rees and Eackernagel,

> Municipalities today are under pressure to deliver more services with fewer resources. In these circumstances conventional economic development initiatives [*i.e.* accumulation models] look the more attractive to all levels of government. At the limit of carrying capacity, however, growth for the sake of additional revenues is both an economic and ecological negative-sum game (Reese and Eackernagel).

Ideally, therefore, all development, including heritage-culture tourist development, should be seeking an "optimal scale" relationship with its host community. That is, a tourist economy of such scale and composition that is compatible with the resource base, personal and social relations, and the ideals, values, and culture of the host society.

The Power of the Local

Another consideration in evaluating potential tourist strategies is that, in a globalizing world, there is a growing demand for commodities and experiences that reflect the local and the unique. Many tourists have always sought out the "authentic" in an attempt at escaping the mediocrity and kitsch of mass-tourism. The privileging of the power of the "local" is central to the concept of "glocalization."

This clever neologism captures that relationship between the nurturing of the local at a time of the assertion of the global, both in culture and in economy (Swyngedouw, 1992, 1992a, 2000; Courchene, 1995, 2001; Featherstone *et al.*, 1995). For Robertson, glocalization is not only the "compression of the world as a whole" and the "linking of localities," it also involves the 'invention' of locality, in the same general sense as the idea of the invention of tradition (Hobsbawm and Ranger, 1983), as well as its 'imagination' (cf. Anderson, 1983). There is indeed currently something like an 'ideology of home' which has in fact come into being partly in response to the constant repetition and global diffusion of the claim that we now live in a condition of homelessness or rootlessness (Robertson, 1995:35).

Moving from the metaphysical to the pragmatic, however, Robertson relates the praxis of glocalization to the economic strategy of "micromarketing." That is, the production of goods and services on a global scale to the particular conditions of local markets:

> glocalization...involves *the construction* of increasingly differentiated consumers, the invention of 'consumer traditions' (of which tourism, arguably the biggest 'industry' of the contemporary world, is undoubtedly

the most clear example). To put it very simply diversity sells (Robertson, 1995:28-29).

That is, rather than globalization producing sameness, the local is the key site for *place marketeers and place entrepreneurs* to gain advantage in an international competitive environment. From this perspective, the *global* and the *local* are intertwined and mutually constituted; global processes influence local actions and prompt reactions. At the same time, local coalitions of financial and political actors are assuming a lot more power to regulate their local economies as well and set objectives that are place specific and maximize unique histories and assets of local places.

In the cultural domain, however, the problem moves beyond the economics of niche-marketing. Processes of time-space compression and cultural homogenization have contributed to a reaffirmation of place-based identities and local loyalties (Harvey, 1989, 1993; Massey, 1991; Zukin, 1991; Smith and Bender, 2001). The particularities of distinct places have been produced by highly localized spatial and social practices over time and globalization has often generated a nostalgic longing for the ever-shrinking space of these distinctive lived experiences (Boym, 2001). Accordingly, faced with political and social change, identity politics become centred on particular sites of meaning where geographically based imaginations have to engage in what Soja has called "the simultaneity and interwoven complexity of the social, the historical and the spatial" (Soja, 1996:261).

The power of distinctive place emerges out of the synergy between time and space, stories and locale, history and geography (Osborne, 2001, 2002a, 2002b). Time is culturally embedded in places and social memory and a sense of place have enhanced cultural continuity, meaning and identity. Further, the latter are not fixed but are a series of constantly shifting stories adjusting to a dynamic external world. And it is historicised space/place that anchors time and where cultures find meaning in what Nuttall calls *memoryscapes* (Nuttall, 1992:54).

Such ideas are similar to Halbwach's *landmarks* (1951), Nora's *lieux de memoire* (1996, 1997, 1998) and Certeau's vision of "practiced place" (1984). For Lefebvre, spaces are "inscriptions in the similarity of the external world of a series of times...the deployment of time" (1995:16) while Bakhtin's concept of chronotope argues that time can be geographically concentrated, a fusion of time and space (Bakhtin, 1981:7).

These various perspectives on the power of place all tend to underscore how *memory places* become crucial when peoples' identities face *dis-placement* or *re-placement*. Such "remembered places" often serve as "symbolic anchors of community" (Gupta and Ferguson, 1992:11) when socio-cultural worlds are being eroded by exogenous forces. People often turn to remembered or imagined places of putative security in a complex and dynamic world. But it is more complex than a return to the familiar worlds of the past. Thus, Meethan queries the quest for the "authentic" past as a "metaphysical search for completeness"; he denies that modernism is inauthentic and unreal; and he argues that what is thought to be authentic in the past is also " a constructed set of values ...[that] cannot be accounted for without considering the social and the material contexts in which it is located" (Meethan, 2001:95). That is, in a globalizing society,

> [t]he increasing commodification of heritage does not render heritage inauthentic, rather it indicates that the production and consumption of heritage is closely tied to the broader issues of politics, the economy and other forms of cultural distinction, and can serve more than one purpose (Meethan, 2001:101-2).

Nevertheless, as Urry has argued, the "interconnections between modernity, identity, and travel and the significance of heritage" underpin tourism as a form of consumption (Urry, 1995:29). That is, heritage-tourism is implicated in formal and informal identity-politics in a dynamic world. Rather than simply travelling across physical space, heritage-cultural tourists are engaged in a metaphysical search for difference — whether it is authentic or not. As Lowenthal put it decades ago, "the past is a foreign country" (1985) and what many modern tourists want, in that wonderful piece of Irish logic, is to "return to place they have never been before."

And some are cashing in on this search for familiar difference. Thus, Italy's "slow food movement" in 1986 was initiated in reaction to the McDonaldisation of local cuisine (Arnot, 2002). A decade later, it has expanded into the *"League of Slow Cities"* with some forty cities trying something different to challenge the effects of globalization. Targetting "discerning tourists," they are marketing themselves as places that are ecologically sensitive, technologically non-intrusive, locally focussed in terms of production and diet, and which celebrate the local rather than the global. They claim to be challenging the "frenetic, ever-quickening pace of living and trying to improve quality of life" (Arnott, 2002). Accordingly, the 10 July 2000 "Manifesto of the League of Slow Cities" speaks of the need for the escape from frenetic modernity by seeking a more tranquil and reflective way. To this end, the "Slow City" movement is attempting to rejuvenate city-life by "time refound":

> Towns and cities packed with squares, theatres, workshops, cafés, restaurants, places of worship, uncontaminated landscapes and the pliers of fascinating crafts. Towns and cities in which man still recognizes the slow, beneficial succession of seasons, the wholesomeness of tasty, healthy produce, the spontaneity of natural rites,

the cult of living tradition and the joy of slow, quiet, reflective living (NPQ, 2000:20).

Looking to "the neo-humanism of the early third millennium," the movement is community-based and shares and acknowledges the distinctive specific qualities of particular places that "create an identity of their own that is visible outside and profoundly felt inside" (NPQ, 2000:20). It is unabashedly a challenge to the ubiquitous threats of a globalization that threatens differences, conceals particular characteristics, and generates mediocrity.

But it is still tourism. It is still the marketing of place. Indeed, it is attempting to maximize the efficiency of the process by targeting high-income tourists and decreasing the pressure on local infrastructures. And in so doing, not only is it enhancing the Quality of Life of permanent residents, it is also acting as an agency of heritage protection and identity formation by celebrating the uniqueness of the local lived-experience, the sense of place.

Lived-in Heritage

But some places are going further. Recognizing the power of the local and the attraction of the distinctive, some historic cities are focusing on the development of distinctiveness for residents and not visitors. In his study of "failed economies" subtitled "The Search for a Value of Place," Power states provocatively, "nobody loves a tourist":

> In fact, most of us have such a strong distaste for the species that we rarely, if ever, consider ourselves part of it. Our aversion to the word *tourist* underlines the incompatibility of conventional mass tourism and local communities. It is also a warning about the political viability of offering tourism as an environmentally benign alternative to extractive activities (Power, 1996:233).

Recognizing the significant material and social costs of a pro-tourist urban strategy, this perspective argues for the promotion of attractions and amenities to induce the infusion of permanent residents and businesses which would stimulate and support economic diversification. For Power, with this as the primary objective, then "if the community cherishes its amenities and has the confidence to protect them, it can lay the foundation for local entrepreneurs to develop compatible, dispersed tourist businesses that help vitalize the economy" (Power, 1996:234). In other words, there are significant economic benefits to be derived from attracting permanent residents: high-income residents with high-order purchases that contribute to the local economy; long-standing contributions to tax-base; the addition of later-life professionals who contribute expertise to the community. And if visitors want to share this enhanced Quality of Life, it can be done by a tourist economy that is "compatible" and "dispersed."

Further, such "Smart Communities" appreciate that by nurturing a distinctive and harmonious lived-in space, they are meeting the locational parameters for many low-impact new-technology industries that are location-flexible. Further, such additions can be compatible with communities' Quality of Life if there is a sensitivity to matters of scale of enterprise, the aesthetics of construction, the compatibility of activity, and the separation of certain function.

It is in this context that R. Florida (2002) speaks of the role of "new culture" and the "creative class" in nurturing human capital, attracting people and, thus, stimulating appropriate growth in urban places. While accommodating the tenets of the Growth Model, therefore, the objective is enhancing Quality of Life for a vibrant and affluent resident urban population, rather than for problematic transients. And for Florida, the key to this strategy is to focus on enhancing the "Quality of Place" by developing the "Power of Place" through the "human capital" theory of regional development (Florida, 2002:215-234). Building on the seminal work of Jane

Jacobs (1961), he asserts that, increasingly, people want to live in places which offer rich lifestyles and opportunities for social inter-action in interesting meeting-points; they are attracted to demo-graphic diversity and that which is authentic not generic; and they want to nurture the need for identity which Castells considers to be diagnostic of peoples' insecurity in an ever-changing postmodern world (Castells, 1997). Taken together, this is what Florida calls "Quality of Place," the spatial rendering of "Quality of Life" (Florida, 2002:231-234). His definition focusses on "the unique set of characteristics that define a place and make it attractive" and it privileges the need for individual and personal engagements with them:

> This is one reason canned experiences are not so popu-lar. A chain theme restaurant, a multimedia-circus sports stadium or a pre-packaged entertainment-and-tourist district is like a packaged tour: You do not get to help create your own experience or modulate the inten-sity; it is thrust upon you (Florida, 2002:232).

For some cities, therefore, theorists are arguing for a focus on quality of lived experience for permanent residents rather than tran-sient tourists. Indeed, for these thinkers, mass-tourism would be antithetic to his "quality of place."

A Shift in Tourism

Finally, the consideration of alternative-tourist and non-tourist strategies is timely as the twenty-first century might be encounter-ing the end of an era of tourism. The origins of modern tourism in the Western world are well documented in its transition from the elite's Grand Tour, to the mass tourism of the newly liberated mass-es, and the emergence of the modern transport-accommodation-entertainment tourist industry. It always had an ocular-focus on sites/sights, reinforced by a taste for the experiential consumption of exotica and erotica. It was further stimulated by the transformation of travel itself from the onerous process of "getting there" to the comfort, and even luxury, of "getting there." Some hotel chains even advertised the attractions of "home away from home."

But is it changing? Is the old paradigm of mass-tourism being challenged by the realities of modern travel: the fear of terrorism; airport and airplane discomfort; fear of SARS, West Nile, and other communicable diseases. For many, their reaction to a destabilized world of travel is to cocoon with home-entertainment stations, home-dining, and home-improvements. And there may be a new era of virtual experience that's displacing the need to touch and see: "Come inside, dear, and watch Mars on TV!"; "I'd rather see the Grand Canyon in the IMAX theatre than walk the southern rim!" Such macro-cultural trends in an insecure world will undoubtedly have an impact on tourist-development strategies.

Whether this is real or not, the post-9/11 reality of the Fourth World War has seen bankrupt air-lines and significant decreases in international travel. To be sure, this has been partly offset by increases in domestic tourism. Nevertheless, the possibility of a shift in tourism practice and demands is sufficiently real to merit consideration. And this too will be part of the dynamic of heritage-cultural strategies for cities seeking economic vitality.

THE SELLING OF KINGSTON

It is in the context of these prevailing discourses that several current models of heritage-tourism in Kingston, Ontario may be recognized.

Like many other cities, Kingston has turned to its inventory of heritage and entertainment resources as part of its economic strategy for the future. It has a rich history, an essentially white-collar and institutional employment structure, diverse social-cultural services and amenities, and an attractive lakeside and countryside location. The cultural-historical mix has generated a townscape that reflects several interest-prompts: Iroquois-Ojibwa First Nations pre-1783; French colonial presence, 1673-1763; British Loyalist military and institutional legacy, 1783-1867; nineteenth century mercantile enterprises and residences, 1783-1880; capital role and associated functions and residences, 1841-43; advent of institutional presence of Penitentiaries, Queen's University, Royal Military College, 1837-present; relics of waterfront commercial and industrial functions, 1851-1950; post-industrial landscape of cultural-heritage development.

Several of the established traditional sites/sights still continue to be vital parts of the city's tourist inventory and economic development strategy: Fort Henry; Bellevue House; Canada's First Capital; the Murney Tower; Hockey Hall of Fame; Marine Museum of the Great Lakes. All of these present the usual array of exhibits, tours, guides, and masses of things to be seen. And the taste for entertainment and fantasy is also being catered to. "Haunted Walks" of Kingston and Fort Henry that offer stories that are "thoroughly researched and will delight even the skeptics," and presented by "local storytellers, dramatists and amateur historians." Together, these attractions, plus the ambience of Kingston, draw some two million visitors who spend some $170 million a year, with a mix of group coach-tours, cruise-boats, individual visits, and some local traffic (RR&C, 2001).

But there is a new initiative. The Kingston Community Strategic Plan refers to its aim of economic prosperity linked to "a vibrant, healthy community" and achieved through "balanced, sustainable growth." It moves the focus of Kingston Economic Development Corporation (KEDCO) away from its initial assertion of tourism as economic multiplier:

> Tourism in the greater Kingston area is vital to many businesses and to the many people who come to the region annually to enjoy its natural beauty, its attrac-

tions and events, its business opportunities ... by attracting visitors to the region, Kingston obtains revenue across a variety of economic sectors including accommodation, restaurants and grocery stores, transportation services, attractions and events, and retail (RR&C 2001:3).

Indeed, in an amalgam of Jacob's, Power's and Florida's emphasis on "quality of place" and Italy's "Slow City Movement," the new Community Strategic Plan calls for:

a safe cohesive community that embraces diversity – a progressive city, built on a human scale, with vibrant organizations and active individuals. We are committed to managing our urban landscape sensibly, encouraging development while protecting our heritage and character of our built and natural environment. We appreciate the importance of parks and open spaces and healthy neighbourhoods supported and linked by transit networks, walking and biking networks (KEDCO, 2002).

Here are all the touch-stones of "Quality of Life" and "Quality of Place": diversity; urban landscape sensitivity; economic development; protection of heritage and the built and natural environment; the importance of parks, open spaces, healthy neighbourhoods; ecologically sensitive transit, walking and biking networks. If only Kingston could discover a distinctive local cuisine and craft industry it would be eligible for the "League of Slow Cities"!

More particularly, tourism is addressed by Kingston's new "Cultural Tourism Initiative" which markets the city's unique combination of urban fabric and townscape, interesting spaces and venues, and quality dining and cultural entertainment (Kingston, 2002). The mission statement reads:

The overall objectives of the Kingston Cultural Initiative are to help the Kingston area thrive as a tourist destination for the arts, heritage and culture, and to develop a cultural business centre - the effect being to enrich the community both through additional economic benefits and new opportunities for cultural growth and expression.

Kingston's "Cultural Covenant" seeks to develop its future as "a community where culture thrives" and which will be recognized as one of North America's most vibrant "cultural business centres characterized by the breadth, scope and scale of its self-sustaining cultural industry". Conforming to Power's melding of economics with a tourism that is sensitive to the host community, the "Covenant" also accommodates Florida's search for the cultural capital of a "creative community" of artists, artisans, scholars, and entrepreneurs and calls for a "community where cultural authenticity and innovation coexist successfully, and where culture is a thread woven into all facets of community life." Further, the "Covenant" has a multidimensional view of culture that includes "performing arts, visual arts, literature, history, architecture and heritage in all its forms."

However, such a forward-looking policy does not eschew the tenets of vague parameters of growth. It is suggested that the success of Kingston's "Cultural Initiative" will render Kingston as a "travel destination" whose "compelling cultural experiences" will attract regional, national and international visitors in "large numbers, year round." Of course, given what has been argued above, this begs the questions "how many?" "what is enough," and is there an optimal traffic for Kingston's urban scale and reception facilities? As always, the philosophy is embedded in the language: tourism is a "business tool" for supporting the development of the "cultural industry"; long-term public benefits will require "sustained investment of public resources" and a "coalition of cultural industry volunteers, community development professionals, and business interests"; if the "economic benefits" of the "cultural industry" are to be realized, the cultural community must adopt a "business ethic" of "managing assets to generate revenue to sustain their activities." Not surprisingly, therefore, the Kingston Economic Development Corporation is advanced as the "Torch bearer" for Kingston's Cultural Initiative.

Clearly, 2003 finds Kingston firmly committed to an economic multiplier model for tourism, albeit one firmly couched in the language and philosophy of nurturing a "quality of place" for residents and visitor's alike. All that has to be considered to ensure a truly flexible posture in a dynamic global-tourism landscape is a recognition that international-tourist flows might be severely disrupted by ongoing international turmoil. But then, to the south lies one of the richest markets in the world!

CONCLUSION AND POSTSCRIPT

The focus of this paper, therefore, is the connection between urban strategies for marketing place, heritage, and cultures. But as Jane Jacobs warned in her *Edge of Empire*, new tourist sites are saturated with the cultural politics of transformation, influenced both by the global and the local (Jacobs, 1996). A decade later, this is more pertinent than ever. Indeed, given challenge to past tourism patterns, the reaction might be a welcome investment in enhancing the attractions of our lived-in places for residents in a new competition between places. The beneficiaries of such a shift will be not only the economic institutions but also the people who consume "Quality of Life" and "Quality of Place." Ironically, Kingston has always been rendered as a "Sleepy Hollow," one of the back-waters of mainstream progress. As the *Toronto Globe* put it on 14 June 1881:

> [Kingston is] a drowsy antiquated place, the relic of a
> past when everybody was not all the time on a jump, but
> took life easily, a land where it is always afternoon, and

people would sooner sit on the wharf and fish than engage in the eternal chase after the dollar.

Perhaps being out of step with past priorities will be of benefit in the future.

Postscript: On 11 April 2003, KEDCO and its "premier tourist partners" announced its newest $200,000 multi-media destination campaign: "Kingston...It's about time!" (KEDCO, 2003). Targeting urban residents, especially in the Greater Toronto Area, the initiative offers "relaxation and time out from busy urban lifestyles." As KEDCO's President put it,

> ...the initiative is very timely given the increasing importance of domestic tourism marketing in major centres such as Toronto. The tourism sector is a significant contributor to the local economy and, by working together, it will become an even greater part of our future.

To this end, "It's about time" promotes the virtues of the Kingston lifestyle for high-income travellers, advertises attractions to be enjoyed at "visitor's chosen pace and taste," provides information to potential new residents for relocating to Kingston, or starting a business. It's coming together at last: "Sleepy Hollow," the "Quality of Place," and the "Smart City" all in one!

End Notes:

[1] Consider the title of the recent conference, "The Tourist Historic City: Sharing Culture for the Future. A Conference on the Significance, Development and Management of Tourism and Culture in Historic Cities and Heritage Locales," Bruges, Belgium, 17-20 March 2002.

[2] A diagnostic of this concern is the initiation of the *Journal of Sustainable Tourism* in 1992.

REFERENCES

Anderson, B. (1991) [1983] *Imagined Communities*, London: Verso.

Anon. (2002) "Slow cities: neo-humanism of the 21st century," *New Perspectives Quarterly*, 17(4):20-21.

Arnot, C. (2002) "Italian towns embrace the idea that slow is beautiful," *Guardian Weekly*, 28 February - 6 March, 28.

Bakhtin, M.M. (1981) "Forms of time and of the chronotope in the novel: notes towards a historical poetics," in M. Holquist (ed.), *The Dialogic Imagination*, Austin: University of Texas Press, 84-258.

Barthel, D. (1996) *Historic Preservation: Collective Memory and Historical Identity*, New Brunswick, N.J.: Rutgers University Press.

Baudrillard, J. (1983) *Simulations*, New York: Semiotext(e).

Bhabha, H. (1990a) "The third space," in J. Rutherford (ed.), *Identity: Community, Culture, Difference*, London: Lawrence and Wishart.

Boym, S. (2001) *The Future of Nostalgia*, New York: Basic Books.

Bramwell, B. and Lane, B. (1999) "Sustainable tourism: contributing to the debates," *Journal of Sustainable Tourism*, 7(1): 1-5.

_____ (2002) "The journal of sustainable development: the first ten years," *Journal of Sustainable Tourism*, 10(1): 1-4.

Butler, R. (1980) "The concept of a tourist area cycle of evolution: implications for management of resources," *Canadian*

Geographer, 24: 5-12.

_____ (1989) "Tourism, heritage and sustainable development," in J. Nelson and S. Woodley (eds.), *Heritage Conservation and Sustainable Development*, Waterloo: Heritage Resources Centre, University of Waterloo, 9-16.

Castells, M. (1997) *The Power of Identity: The Information Age: Economy, Society, and Culture, Vol. I*, Oxford: Blackwell.

Clarke, J. (1997) "A framework of approaches to sustainable tourism," *Journal of Sustainable Tourism*, 5(3): 224-233.

Clifford, J. (1997) *"Diasporas" in Routes: Travel and Translation in the Late Twentieth Century*, Cambridge: Harvard University Press.

Courchene, T. (1995) "Glocalization: The Regional/International Interface", *Canadian Journal of Regional Science*, 18(1): 120.

Courchane, T. (2001) *A State of Minds: Towards a Human Capital Future for Canadians*, Montreal: IRPP.

Daniels, S. (1993) *Fields of Vision: Landscape Imagery and National Identity in England and the United States*, Princeton: Princeton University Press.

Daiches, D. and Flower, J. (1979) *Literary Landscapes of the British Isles: A Narrative Atlas*, New York: Paddington Press.

de Certeau, M. (1984) *The Practice of Everyday Life*, Berkeley: California University Press.

Donald, B. (2001) "Economic competitiveness and quality of place in city regions: a "new" regional growth theory?," *Paper pre-*

sented at Annual Meeting of Canadian Association of Geographers, Montreal.

Faulkner, B. and Tidswell, C. (1997) "A framework for examining community impacts of tourism," Journal of Sustainable Tourism, 5(1): 3-28.

Fawcett, C. and Cormack, P. (2001) "Guarding the authenticity of literary tourism sites," Annals of Tourism Research, 28(3): 686-704.

Herbert, D. (2001) "Literary places, tourism and the heritage experience," Annals of Tourism Research, 28(2): 312-333.

Featherstone, M., Lash, S. and Robertson, R. (eds.) (1995) Global Modernities, Sage: London.

Florida, R. (2002) The Rise of the Creative Class: And How it's Transforming Work, Leisure, Community, and Everyday Life, New York: Basic Books.

Graham, B. Ashworth, G.J. and Tunbridge, J.E. (2000) A Geography of Heritage: Power, Culture and Economy, London: Arnold.

Gupta, A. and Ferguson, J. (1992) "Beyond 'culture': space, identity, and the politics of difference," Cultural Anthropology, 7(1): 6-23.

Hall, S. (1990) "Cultural identity and diaspora", in J. Rutherford (ed.), Identity, Community, Culture, Difference, London: Lawrence and Wishart.

_____ (1991) "The local and the global: globalization and ethnicity," in A.D. King (ed.), Culture, Globalization and the World-

System: Contemporary Questions for the Representation of Identity, Basingstoke: Macmillan.

Hall, S. (1992) "The question of cultural identity," in S. Hall *et al.* (eds.), *Modernity and its Futures*, Cambridge: Polity.

_____ (1996) "Introduction: who needs identity?," in S. Hall and P. du Gay (eds.), *Questions of Cultural Identity*, London: Sage.

Halbwach, M. (1951) *The Collective Memory*, New York: Harper and Row.

Häkli, J. (1999) "Cultures of demarcation: territory and national identity in Finland," in G.H. Herb and D.H. Kaplan (eds.), *Nested Identities: Nationalism, Territory, and Scale*, Lanham: Rowman and Littlefield, 123-150.

Hardy, A.L. and Beeton, R.J.S. (2001) "Sustainable tourism or maintainable tourism: managing resources for more than average outcomes," *Journal of Sustainable Development*, 9(3): 168-192.

Harvey, D. (1988) *The Condition of Post-modernity*, Oxford: Blackwell.

_____ (1993) "Class relations, social justice, and the politics of difference," in M. Keith and S. Pile (eds.), *Place and the Politics of Identity*, London: Routledge.

Hinch, T.D. (1996) "Urban tourism: perspectives on sustainability," *Journal of Sustainable Tourism*, 4(2): 95-110.

Hobsbawm, E. and Ranger, T. (1983) *The Invention of Tradition*, Cambridge: University of Cambridge Press.

Hunter, M. (1996) *Preserving the Past: The Rise of Heritage in Modern Britain*, Stroud: Alan Sutton.

Jacobs, J. (1961) *The Death and Life of Great American Cities*, New York: Random House.

_____ (1996) *Edge of Empire: Postcolonialism and the City*, New York: Routledge.

Jansen-Verbeke, M. (1997) "Urban tourism: managing resources and visitors," in S. Wabab and J. Pigram (eds.), *Tourism Development and Growth: The Challenge of Sustainability*, London: Routledge, 237-256.

_____ (1998) "Tourisimification of historical cities," *Annals of Tourist Research*, 25(3): 739-742.

Jansen-Verbeke, M. and Lievois, E. (1999) "Analysing heritage resources for urban tourists in European cities," in D.G. Pearce and R.W. Butler (eds.), *Contemporary Issues in Tourism Development: Analysis and Applications*, London: Routledge, 81-107.

Kearns, G. and Philo, C. (eds.) (1993) *Selling Places: The City as Cultural Capital, Past and Present*, Oxford: Pergammon Press.

KEDCO (2003) Press Release: "It's About Time...City's Largest Tourism Marketing Campaign Unveiled," Kingston Economic Development Corporation, 11 April 2003.

Kingston (2002) kingstonculture.com.

Lefebvre, H. (1991) *The Production of Space*, Oxford: Blackwell.

Lowenthal, D. (1985) *The Past is a Foreign Country*, Cambridge:

Cambridge University Press.

_____ (1996) *Possessed by the Past: The Heritage Crusade and the Spoils of History*, New York: The Free Press.

Massey, D. (1991) "The political place of locality studies," *Environment and Planning A*, 23: 267-81.

May, J. and Thrift, N. (2001) *Timespace: Geographics of Temporality*, London: Routledge.

Meethan, K. (2001) *Tourism in Global Society: Place, Culture, Consumption*, Houndmills: Palgrave.

Mitchell, C.J.A. (1998) "Entrepreneurialism, commodification and creative destruction: a model of post-modern community development," *Journal of Rural Studies*, 14: 273-86.

Mitchell, C.J.A., Atkinson, R.G. and Clark, A. (2001) "The creative destruction of Niagara-on-the-Lake," *The Canadian Geographer*, 45(2): 285-299.

Nora, P. (1996) *Realms of Memory: The Construction of the French Past. Vol. I: Conflicts and Divisions; 1997. Realms of Memory: The Construction of the French Past. Vol. II: Traditions; 1998. Realms of Memory: The Construction of the French Past. Vol. III: Symbols*, New York: Columbia University Press.

Osborne, B. (2001) "Landscapes, memory, monuments, and commemoration: putting identity in its place," *Canadian Ethnic Studies*, Vol. XXXIII(3): 39-77.

Osborne, B. (2002) "Locating identity: landscapes of memory," *Choice*, 39(11/12): 1903-1911.

Osborne. B.S. (2002) "The place of memory and identity," *Diversities*, 1:1(Summer): 9-13.

_____ (2002a) "Moose Jaw's 'great escape': constructing tunnels, deconstructing heritage, marketing places," *Material History Review*, Spring: 16-28.

Palmer, J.P. (2002) "Bread and circuses: the local benefits of sports and cultural businesses," C.D. Howe Institute, Commentary, *Urban Papers*, 161(March): 1-18.

Power, T.M. (1996) *Lost Landscapes and Failed Economies: The Search for a Value of Place*, Washington D.C.: Island Press.

Pryce, P. (1999) *'Keeping the Lakes' Way': Reburial and the Re-creation of a Moral World among an Invisible People*, Toronto: University of Toronto Press.

Robertson, R. (1995) "Glocalization: time-space and homogeneity-heterogeneity," in M. Featherstone, S. Lash and R. Robertson (eds.), *Global Modernities*, Sage: London, 25-44.

Robins, K. (1991) "Tradition and translations: national culture in a global context," in J. Corner and S. Harvey (eds.), *Enterprise and Heritage*, London: Routledge.

RR&C (2001) *An Overvew of Tourism in the Kingston Area: An Analysis of Domestic & International Travel Surveys (1999)*, Kingston: Kingston Economic Development Corporation (KEDCO).

Rutherford, J. (ed.) (1990) *Identity, Community, Culture, Difference*, London: Lawrence and Wishart.

Shaffer, M.S. (2001) *See America First: Tourism and National Identity*, Washington: Smithsonian Institution Press.

Sharpley, R. (2000) "Tourism and sustainable development: exploring the theoretical divide," *Journal of Sustainable Tourism*, 8(1): 1-19.

Smith, S.J. (1999) "The cultural politics of difference," in D. Massey *et al.* (eds.), *Human Geography Today*, Cambridge: Polity.

Soja, E. (1999) "Thirdspace: expanding the scope of the geographic imagination," in D. Massey *et al.* (eds.), *Human Geography Today*, Cambridge: Polity.

_____ (1996) *Thirdspace: Journeys to Los Angeles and Other Real-and-Imagined Places*, Oxford: Blackwell.

Smith, M.P. and Bender, T. (eds.) (2001) "City and nation: rethinking place and identity", *Comparative Urban and Community Research*, 7: New Brunswick and London.

Squire, S.J. (1994) "The cultural values of literary tourism," *Annals of Tourism Research*, 21: 103-120.

Swyngedouw, E. (1992) "Territorial organization and the space/technology nexus", *Transactions, I.B.G. NS*, 17: 417-33.

_____ (1992) "The mammon quest: 'glocalisation', interspatial competition and the monetary order: the construction of new scales," in M. Dunford and G. Kafkalas (eds.), *Cities and Regions in the New Europe: The Global Local Interplay and Spatial Development Strategies*, London: Belhaven Press.

_____ (2000) "Elite power, global forces, and the political economy of 'glocal' development", in G.L. Clark, M.P. Feldman and M.S. Gertler (eds.), *The Oxford Handbook of Economic Geography*, Toronto: Oxford University Press.

Tunbridge J.E. and Ashworth, G.J. (1996) *Dissonant Heritage: The Management of the Past as a Resource in Conflict*, Toronto: John Wiley.

Urry, J. (1995) *Consuming Places*, London: Routledge.

Zukin, S. (1991) *Landscapes of Power: From Detroit to Disney World*, Berkeley: University of California Press.

8

Japanese Tourism and the Japanese Market

Atsuko Hashimoto

INTRODUCTION

It is vital for a tourism destination to target the right kind of market so that the benefits to the destination can be optimized. The type of tourism product the destination can offer also affects the type of tourists they can lure. However, without careful consideration and planning, the destination might be attracting tourists who bring little benefit to the destination. Public and quasi-public National Tourism Organizations (NTOs) such as Ministries of Tourism, Destination Marketing Organizations, and Regional Tourism Promotion Offices often have influence over private businesses and other stakeholders as to what types of target markets are desirable. To select a most desirable target market, market research, statistics, and demographic and psychographic profiling of target markets are unquestionably important. Using the example of Japanese tourists, this chapter will illustrate, how detailed market research can generate rich information that NTOs and even private entrepreneurs can use to identify, entice and motivate selected target markets to benefit the destination.

CONSUMER ANALYSES

In most market analyses, segmentation is a vital concept. Segmentation research is often conducted to address and improve marketing problems such as sales, market share, and cost-effectiveness of advertisements; meanwhile it also addresses consumer behaviour such as the selection of tourism products and spending patterns (Smith, 1995). However, when it comes to industry-oriented information sources such as NTOs' tourism statistics and figures, information is predominantly about the tourist arrival numbers, estimates of tourist spending (expenditure), and length of stay, which can be numerically recorded. Even if there are some demographic and psychographic information added, such as in the case of Tourism White Paper published by Japanese government (MLIT, 2006a; b), the information traditionally does not go beyond the description of life styles, *e.g.*, familiarity with internet promotion materials, high VFR rates and travel restrictions. Although such demographic and psychographic information is undoubtedly useful to grasp factors influencing current tourism activities, more detailed market research, especially in the areas of culture, tradition, social pressures and norms, will help to explain the tourists' behaviour in the destination and will provide an added advantage to the destination in its marketing and management. This detailed information will better prepare the destination to handle tourists' culture-bound behaviours and preferences regarding services and souvenirs.

Japanese Tourists to Canada

In many destinations, Japanese tourists have been known as organized tourists, circuit travellers, having high spending power, and demanding a high standard of service and comfort. For the purpose of rectifying trade surpluses, the Japanese government encouraged their citizens to travel abroad in 1986 and since then the number of Japanese outbound tourists has been steadily increasing. Canada has been targeting the Japanese market with keen interest. Japan has been Canada's second largest trading partner since 1973 (The Canadian Trade Commissioner Service, 2006) and one of the leading sources of overseas tourism income. In 2004-2005 an estimated 84.5 per cent of Overnight Tourist Revenues came from US and Interprovincial Canadian tourists; of the rest (Europe and other Overseas markets), Japan is the second largest revenue contributor after the UK (Canadian Tourism Commission, 2006). The Canadian Tourism Commission has been conducting continuous dialogue with the Japanese Tourism Industry in the form of the "Canada-Japan Tourism Conference" which started in 1993. The 9th Conference was held in 2004 in Banff, and the 10th Conference in

Nagoya in 2006. This conference is to develop mutual interests in better partnerships and an increase in visitor numbers for both countries (Koumelis, 2006; Tourism Staff, Feb. 2006; Tourism Staff, July 2006; CTC, 2006; Canadian Tourism Commission, 2000a).

Statistical Significance of Japanese Market to Canadian Tourism

As an economic activity, tourism is expected to bring in substantial economic gains and the Japanese market is considered to be one of the leading sources of overseas tourism revenue. The Canadian Tourism Commission and Statistics Canada divide tourism statistics by world regions. Among the European markets to Canada, the UK tourist arrival number and the revenue from the UK tourists are the highest. Japan, the leading figure in the group from the Asia Pacific Region, follows the UK trends compared to the rest of the Asia Pacific Region. Japan also exceeds the second and the third European tourist generating countries, namely France and Germany (Table 8.1, 8.2).

Following the turbulent years of early 2000, the tourist arrival numbers to Canada fluctuated drastically. After the 9/11 terrorist attacks in the United States, tourists from Europe continuously declined in 2002. Canadian tourism suffered a decline from SARS in the year 2003. The Japanese market to Canada showed nearly a 50 per cent decline in tourist arrival numbers in 2003. On the other hand, when Canada was officially cleared of SARS in 2004, the recovery rate of the Japanese market growth was a phenomenal 65.8 per cent increase over 2003. The total revenue from Overseas Tourism directly links to the tourist arrival numbers. Table 8.1 summarizes the fluctuations of tourism revenues from Canada's Top Four Markets.

Table 8.1: Tourist Revenue ($ million Cdn) from the Top Four Markets

	2002	01/02 change	2003	02/03 change	2004	03/04 change	2005	04/05 change
UK	993	(-3.3)	945	(-4.8)	1129	(19.5)	1300	(15.1)
Japan	666	(5.3)	348	(-47.7)	577	(65.8)	600	(4.0)
France	374	(-14.2)	365	(-2.8)	441	(20.8)	500	(13.4)
Germany	385	(-15.3)	345	(-10.4)	408	(18.3)	400	(-2.0)

Source: Canadian Tourism Commission, 2004; 2005; 2006.

As shown in Table 8.2, Canada's Top Four Markets generally decreased in arrival numbers and total spending in the year 2003. Although other countries never replaced those four markets, the Japanese market clearly showed its vulnerability towards instability (in this case SARS) and dropped from second place to fourth place. Nonetheless, when examining tourists' spending per night, Japanese tourists are the highest spenders among the four key markets even in the year 2003. Likewise, spending per trip also illustrates that the Japanese tourists are spending the highest amount per trip. Analyses of spending per trip or per night are often neglected in the "Facts and Figures" type of information, yet it is useful to identify which individual tourist is able to spend more (*i.e.* from Table 8.2 a Japanese tourist spends close to 50 per cent more than a French tourist per night). For that reason, the Japanese market has become a desirable market to Canada and the Canadian Trade Commissioner Service (2006) calls the Japanese market "Canada's largest source of overseas tourism revenue".

Table 8.2: Top Four Overseas Markets to Canada

	Key Markets	Trips ('000)	Nights ('000)	Spending ($ mill Cdn)	Spending per trip	Spending per night
2002	UK	721	9371	993	1377.25	105.95
	Japan	423	4884	666	1574.47	136.36
	France	312	4144	374	1198.72	90.25
	Germany	292	4319	385	1318.49	89.14
2003	UK	691	8961	945	1367.58	105.46
	France	275	4180	365	1327.27	87.32
	Germany	253	3942	345	1363.63	87.52
	Japan	250	2994	348	1392.00	116.23
2004	UK	801	10221	1115	1392.01	109.09
	Japan	391	4742	553	1414.32	116.62
	France	337	4742	553	1414.32	116.62
	Germany	296	4588	397	1341.22	86.53

Source: Statistics Canada, 2003; 2004; 2005.

History of Recent Japanese Tourism

Japanese outbound tourism reached a peak in 2000 with the total number of outbound tourists at over 17.8 million Affected by world incidents, in the following few years there was a drop in the number and in 2005 the number of outbound tourists recovered to 17.4 million. Table 8.3 details some of the key events in Japanese tourism over the last 40 years (Table 8.3).

Table 8.3: Summary of the Recent History of Japanese Tourism

Year	Events
1964	Tokyo Olympics - liberation of air transport (cheaper seats), passport issuing process became easier
1986	Ministry of Transport of Japan launched the **Ten Million Program** (a 5-year plan)
1990	Reached ten million in 1990 (one year earlier than planned)
1991	Ministry of Transport launched **Two-Way Tourism 21**
1993	**Two Million Visitor Two-Way Tourism Challenge** plan was agreed between Canada and Japan • By 1999, Japanese visitors to Canada is at 35 per cent of objective, Canadian visitors to Japan is at 22 per cent of objective. • Extend time frame to 2010, downsizing the challenge to 1.5 million, and extended period to 2010 to meet the 2-million challenge.
1999	Japanese Government implemented **Welcome Plan 21** • plan to double inbound tourism to Japan
2003	Japanese Government launched the **Visit Japan Campaign** • Target 10 million inbound tourists to Japan by 2010 • US/Canada market: "Japanese culture and traditions" and "nature" for senior market; "animé" and "games" for youth market
2006	10th Canada-Japan Tourism Conference (Nagoya, Japan) • The 2010 visitation targets of 200,000 Canadians travelling to Japan and 800,000 Japanese travelling to Canada

Source: MLIT, 2006a, b; Tourism Staff, July 2006; Canadian Tourism Commission, 2000a; b; c.

Both Inbound and Outbound travel became accessible to the general population in 1964 in the year of the Tokyo Olympics through more affordable airline tickets and a loosening of travel restrictions and regulations. In this year, the total number of outbound tourists was 128,000, mostly business travellers, while the number of inbound tourists to Japan was 353,000. In 1971, the number of outbound tourists surpassed the number of inbound tourists (961,000 and 661,000 respectively). In 1986, Japan was enjoying a strong Yen and the government launched the Ten Million Program to encourage Japanese outbound tourism to reduce the trade surplus. The Ten Million Program aimed to send ten million Japanese tourists to foreign destinations by 1991. However, with a strong Yen, a more affluent, younger generation and seniors market, and government support prompting overseas travels, the target was reached in 1990. Since then, Japanese outbound tourism steadily and considerably increased. In 1990, the number of Japanese outbound tourists was 11 million, while the number of inbound tourists was 3.2 million.

In order to balance inbound and outbound tourism, the Japanese government launched a series of programmes. The "Welcome Plan 21" program started in 1991 to attract more inbound tourists. The Japan National Tourism Organization (JNTO) led the Two-Way Tourism project with specific destinations including Canada. In the Two-Way Tourism project, the JNTO and the partner NTOs/DMOs came up with strategies and target numbers to balance inbound-outbound tourism for both parties. A "New Welcome Plan 21" came forth in 2000 to emphasize more countryside and alternative destinations in Japan: the Japanese government launched the Visit Japan Campaign with a logo of "Yokoso! Japan" in 2003, thus more vigorously enticing inbound tourists to Japan. In 2005, the number of Japanese outbound tourists was 17.4 million, and the number of inbound tourists was 6.7 million (MLIT, 2006a). The Campaign's target is to increase the inbound tourists to Japan to 10 million by 2010. As a Two-Way Tourism partner, Canada and Japan have recently agreed that both parties will work toward the 2010 targets of 200,000 Canadians travelling to Japan and 800,000 Japanese travelling to Canada (Tourism Staff, July 2006).

Understanding the Japanese Market

After the 9/11 terrorist attacks in the United States in 2001, the Japanese were concerned about travelling through US airports to get to Canada. In addition, the SARS outbreak in 2003 and the Canadian beef ban based on cases of Mad Cow Disease somewhat tarnished Canada's reputation of having high standards of hygiene and health. Despite the fact that Canada has done many public relations and promotional events to recover the reputation as a safe destination, Japanese tourists are still overly concerned about their safety. In addition to their concerns over safety, spending extra time going through airport security systems is another de-motivating factor, particularly for North American destinations. It is also noted that oil price hikes since Hurricane Katrina in 2005 and unceasing conflicts in the Middle East have affected the price of travel. These factors need to be analysed at a deeper level to understand the underlying reasons why fewer Japanese tourists chose Canada as a destination.

External Factors

There are factors occurring physically, structurally or politically that are beyond an individual person's control. These external factors, nevertheless, have an inevitable influence not only on an individual's decision making on holidays and their spending of money, but also on the lifestyles and the "stages of life" individuals go through.

1. Economic Factors

The Japanese economy has been in a slump for the past 15 years. The initial hit of economic recession was in February 2000, which yielded the worst unemployment rate since 1953 when such statistics began to be collected. Initially it was more a psychological shock than an actual financial loss, yet after enjoying a so-called "economic bubble" period, the impact was substantial. Since then, the economy has suffered from repeated smaller waves of economic recession. Corporations' structural changes cost not only jobs but also many lives; the cutting down of positions means more work load and demands on fewer people in the work force; consequently the work force is experiencing a "burn out" syndrome both in terms of mental and physical health. These factors have led to even shorter holidays (McCurry, 2005; Okubo, 2005; Personal Communication, 2006a; b; c; d), and therefore long haul trips are not favoured. The series of economic recessions inevitably caused psychological and attitudinal changes in preferences for pastime activities. This will be examined later in the chapter.

With recessions and organizational restructuring, and IT-related entrepreneurship and business ventures, the gap between high income and low income groups has been widening. With increasing mistrust and disloyalty to "corporations" and "companies", younger generations prefer not to dedicate their lives to one organization as their predecessors did and choose part-time status called "Freeters"[1]. Freeters do not receive work benefits, compensation or good wages, however the lack of responsibility, lack of commitment, and flexibility of work are the reasons why younger generations are choosing to be Freeters. This low-income level stratum is alarmingly increasing; there is estimated to be over 3 million Freeters today and many of them are well into the 30s (Personal Communication, 2006b; d). The Freeters do not have enough disposal income for long-haul overseas travel and they are unable to start their own household or careers.

In the past, overseas travel was popular as domestic tours used to be more expensive than short-haul overseas tours. It is still true to a certain extent that Asian destinations can offer cheaper packages than domestic packages. However, the domestic destinations are regaining their popularity as social attitudes towards overseas travel as "prestige" is weakening. Such phenomena are triggered by psychological changes associated with the economic situation and changes in values over the past decade or so.

In addition, fuel surcharge hikes on airfares due to a shortage of crude oil after Hurricane Katrina, the US's war in Iraq, and increasing conflicts in the Middle East countries are all negatively affecting travel expenses. Japanese travel intermediaries began to collect a "fuel charge" in addition to airfare in late 2004. For instance, when the special rate campaign for airfare between Tokyo and Los Angeles was 30,000 yen (CDN $300), the consumer had to add another 30,000 yen for the fuel charge and related taxes. Although the total costs could still be a good bargain, such "additional" costs are de-motivating rather than enticing (Personal Communication, 2006c).

2. Political Factors

Political factors easily affect the Japanese market's movement. For instance, the Ten Million Progam was welcomed in 1986 by potential Japanese market segments who needed "official" support to take longer holidays. Tourism development policy in Japan is currently part of the government's regional economic development strategy to encourage more domestic and inbound tourism. The authoritarian nature of the Japanese culture is clearly observed in the way Japanese obey government policy of the time without question.

On the negative side, political upheavals in or near destinations can easily affect the Japanese market. In particular, terrorism-related attacks to tourist sites, facilities and on modes of transportation lead to a self-imposed ban on certain destinations. The Japanese are extremely conscious of "safety" and "hygiene" in their daily lives. Before the Irish Republican Army (IRA) agreed to a cease fire, the UK and Ireland were not popular destinations and today repeated Al-Qaida related terrorism acts deter Japanese to travel to certain European countries and the United States. The Middle East attracts a very small number of Japanese tourists due to its on-going conflicts.

The Japanese government are also quick to respond to outbreaks of illness and epidemics such as SARS, Foot-and-Mouth Disease, Avian Flu, along with Cholera, Malaria and Typhoid in destinations. Government warnings over these issues will keep the Japanese market away from the area for a considerable length of time.

3. Social Factors

Media and opinion leaders (*e.g.*, experts, celebrities and politicians) determine what is fashionable and what is not in Japan. Authorities' opinions easily sway the Japanese. Presently the Japanese media is focusing on heritage, traditions and history. A variety of current TV shows are based on these themes (Personal Communication, 2006c, d). Travel magazines and web media are also promoting destinations with history and heritage. Many European countries and Asian countries with rich history and traditions are favoured. New World destinations cannot provide such products that can compete with Old World destinations.

Media do not necessarily focus on tourist destinations. Nevertheless, broadcasting and featuring East Asian films, TV shows, entertainment programmes, that introduce celebrities from Asian countries have a profound influence on Japanese interests in these countries. The interactions and featured travels of entertainment celebrities from different Asian countries to other Asian countries have had positive results generating interest and favourable views towards Asian cultures, heritage and history among younger generations (Personal Communication, 2006b). In the last few years, China and Korea are becoming quite fashionable and the trend is towards short break travel focused on these countries (Personal Communication, 2006b, c, d).

Another social factor is the social acceptance towards travelling. The Japanese are known for their workaholic tendencies and this has always been an obstacle for taking holidays. Rebuilding the Japanese Post-war economy drove Japanese to the collective understanding that non-productive activities such as "taking a holiday" must be disallowed, even when the Japanese economy entered the stage of excessive trade surplus. Overwork without compensation and weekend work were the norm and most of the employees did not use their entitled paid holidays. With the Government's support for the Ten Million Program, implementing a two-day weekend for schools and introducing long weekend Mondays, Japanese employees were forced to get used to the idea of "taking a holiday" without feeling ostracised. Today the workforce situation has changed direction again and the split between Freeters and overloaded full-time employees is widening, creating a rift between them. The Health and Welfare Ministry of Japan will introduce a law in 2007 to compel firms to oversee that their full-time employees do take all their entitled paid holidays (McCurry, 2006).

Life stage is another factor. Japan is facing a serious issue that the people in their prime age for careers are the overloaded employees who are too busy to take a holiday and start their own family, or are the Freeters who do not have enough financial resources to take a holiday and start their own family. Late marriage is also causing a delay in events of the adulthood life stage (*e.g.*, employment, family life and empty nest) as the people in their 40s for example are busy with child rearing with children under 12 years old. This leaves women who are married without their own careers and without yet having their own children to care for, or those who have finished child rearing but with husbands that are still too busy working, as a prime target market for overseas travel. These combined factors further restrict the actual market available to travel.

Social changes are also clearly affecting Japanese women of marriageable age. A recent survey by a major Japanese newspaper company revealed that 73 per cent of single female respondents and 67 per cent of single male respondents think that women can be happy living on their own (BBC, 2005). Sociologist Masahiro Yamada coined the term "parasite singles" to describe "young people who sponge off their parents and use their rent-free incomes to splurge on designer goodies, expensive dinners and trips abroad" (Wiseman, 2004). The Japanese Institute of Life Insurance's survey also found that 54 per cent of women in their late 20s are still single, 50 per cent of single women aged 35 to 54 have no intention to marry; and in 1997, 77.7 per cent of single twenty-something women were the happiest people – they were content with their lives (Wiseman, 2004). These young women are the ones who have enough income for brand goods shopping and numerous overseas trips with other female friends, colleagues and family members.

The year 2007 is when a large portion of the Baby Boomer workforce will retire. The first wave of Baby-boomers (born 1947-49) is estimated to be 6.91 million (5.4 per cent of total population) (Nitta, 2006). This elderly generation holds higher financial assets than any other generation and have the highest consumption patterns; this is simply the people over 60 years old (retirement age) who have finished paying their mortgages as well as paying for the education and necessities for children. They spend mostly on travel, medication and renovation of houses (Nitta, 2006). The benefits of these baby-boomers to the travel industry have already been experienced; in 2004, the cruise industry enjoyed a 25 per cent increase in passengers (Web Japan, 2005). The Baby-boomers tend to travel as a couple, have an inclination towards Special Interest Tours and towards new or less-known destinations (Web Japan 2005; Nitta, 2006).

Internal Factors

Social and psychological factors are usually influenced by external factors such as economic downturns. When the economy fluctuates and organizational re-structuring affects the workforce and work patterns, taking a holiday is not fully appreciated by society. The workaholic tendency in Japanese society cannot be changed overnight. With change in the perceived reduced economic power of individual Japanese, the types of recreational activities that are undertaken has also changed over the last decade or so. How individuals spend money also has changed. Some of these aspects will be examined below.

1. Disapproval of the concept of taking a holiday.

Although the government is trying to encourage Japanese to take their entitled paid holidays and weekends off, Japanese men especially cannot tolerate the two-day weekend and many men end up going into their offices on Saturdays. It is considered normal for many Japanese to work 6 days a week while self-employed people work seven days a week. Many companies do not provide sick leave so some employees have to use their own annual holiday time to cover when they are sick. There was an attempt to make schoolchildren take alternative Saturdays off, yet this will soon be cancelled as society observed a discernable decline in the academic achievements of schoolchildren. School summer holidays are 40 days, yet many older children attend summer schools or cram schools during the summer holiday period.

Many middle-aged people and those from the older generation still believe that taking a holiday is unproductive, causing a great deal of trouble for colleagues and neighbours, and that their taking a holiday does not contribute to society. The only time one can take more than a 7-day holiday without bitter remarks from colleagues and neighbours is a honeymoon trip (Hashimoto, 1992). Among the younger generation, the physical constraints of prolonged work hours and accumulating fatigue do not allow the younger generation to consider holiday taking attractive (Personal communication 2006a; c; d).

2. Social obligation, feeling of guilt, and souvenir shopping.

In general, everything is expensive in Japan due to the extremely high price of land. One square metre of land in the Ginza district in Tokyo cost US $163000 in 2005 (BBC, 2006). This pushes the cost of labour high and consequently everything becomes very expensive. Many people who are working in the Metropolitan Tokyo area are unable to purchase a single-family house within a two-hour commuting distance (Hashimoto, 1992; 2000). With the high cost of housing, a large number of Japanese used their disposable income for traveling or other types of hobbies and for recreation-related expenses instead of purchasing a house during the bubble economy. As the economy has now hit more difficult times, even this use of disposable income for travel has been reduced. Even after a couple of decades of having overseas travels encouraged, the society does not fully accept the notion of holiday taking, and those who take days off to go abroad feel obliged to buy some souvenirs for their colleagues who are covering for them during their absence. Souvenirs are regarded as a token of thanks and an apology for causing inconvenience through absence (Hashimoto, 1992; 2000). Japanese tourists are known to purchase large quantities of small souvenir items or relatively expensive gifts such as bottles of ice wine. Due to customs regulations (limits of duty free goods) and often tight travel itineraries, Japanese tourists tend to seek small souvenirs that are easy to carry and yet are of high value (rare, limited versions, geographically fixed, and/or expensive) (Hashimoto, 1992; 2000; Telfer and Hashimoto, 2000).

Japanese traditionally used gift-giving customs to maintain good human relationships. Today, the price or value of the gift is used as a barometer to measure the sincerity of the gift giver. However, the recent economic recession caused a reflective change in shopping behaviours, particularly in women's shopping behaviours for their own use. Two decades ago the trend in shopping was "brand goods" from Europe (see details in Hashimoto, 1992; 2000). The trend today is "real value for money". The brand name or price is no longer an indicator of value or class; whatever has the best value to the purchaser is worthy of acquiring. Today's Japanese female tourists hold their purse string tight (Personal communication, 2006b).

3. Overseas travel as social status.
After the Second World War, Japanese social class was almost completely abolished and monetary wealth became a symbol of social status. Although the price of overseas travel is coming down, many

middle aged and older Japanese consider overseas travel as a "once in a lifetime" experience. They take many photographs or video record the places they visit not only to remember the places, but as evidence that they have actually been there (Hashimoto, 1992; 2000). This is still true in the case of Japanese tourists from relatively remote areas. However, mainstream tourists from urban areas no longer consider overseas travel as a form of prestige. Recently promoted destinations are concentrated in the Asian neighbourhood and short breaks to closer destinations with rich historical legacies are gaining in popularity (Personal communication, 2006b; c; d). Japanese tourists from urban areas tend to be experienced tourists. Therefore, rather than circuiting several countries within an 8-day itinerary, these experienced tourists tend to choose one or two favourite places to visit, make excursions from a base location, and enjoy unearthing treasures of locally-made crafts and knickknacks (Personal communication, 2006b).

There are numerous theme parks in Japan, which simulate European and American worlds (Hamilton-Oehrl, 1998). Japanese have a deep-rooted inferiority complex against white Caucasian dominant societies because the Japanese first encounters with Europeans were in 1542, when the Portuguese brought guns and Christianity. The Dutch brought western medicine and the British brought education. American Commodore Perry forced the Japanese by arms to open the country to the outside world in 1854. Those Europeans came to Japan as fearful masters and teachers. On the other hand, the neighbouring Asian cousins share a more similar culture and beliefs, and the Japanese have even tried to colonize some of these countries. During the course of history, the Japanese failed to see other Asian countries as attractive, exotic and superior or equal to the Japanese society (Hashimoto, 1992; 2000). Nevertheless over the last five years the trend has shifted. The Japanese longing for visiting Europe and North America was supported by the travel industry while Japan enjoyed the bubble economy. Long-haul and more expensive prestigious tours to Europe added social status. The unstable economic situations in the past five years or so have shaken the Japanese sense of economic power and created a re-focusing on the Asian neighbourhood, drawing attention to "new" destinations.

4. Obsession for hygiene and the purity of the group.

The Japanese are known to be obsessed with hygiene. For over a decade, many Japanese tourists have been using anti-bacterial wet tissues to clean toilet seats in public washrooms. This obsession with hygiene extends to mental hygiene. The average Japanese is afraid of being contaminated by the outside world, including ideas and customs. If they import a new idea from a foreign country, it has to be modified, changed and processed before it is completely accepted. During a short trip abroad, the Japanese tourists cannot go through this purification process for ideas and customs from foreign countries. Apart from the practical reasons that many of them do not speak foreign languages and are unfamiliar with the destination, one subconscious reason for joining an all-inclusive package tour, run by a Japanese tour operator, is to minimize the chance of contamination (Hashimoto, 1992). Hotels are carefully selected to satisfy Japanese high expectations of "hygiene and sanitation" and high "service standards". Japanese-speaking tour guides, preferably of Japanese origin, are assigned to each tour group. Even "customized" mass tourists or Foreign Independent Travel (FIT) who use Air-Hotel packages feel more safe and secure while travelling within the familiar environmental bubble of "Japanese-ness".

As was previously noted, Japanese tourists are becoming more experienced and there is an increase in demand for "tailored" or "independent" travel. Special interest tours that attract middle-aged tourists who prefer to go to places such as Nepal for mountain hiking rather than hiking in Japan (Personal communication, 2006c) are one example of a special interest tour increasing in popularity. Yet, these adventure tourists are guided by Japanese-speaking guides and stay in comfortable accommodations if not in a well-equipped base camp, having porters (often called "sherpas") to carry necessary loads. A very small number of Japanese tourists can truly break away from the environmental bubble and be a totally independent tourist.

5. Changing trends and women.

Japanese society historically accepted that married women are in charge of the domestic domain. This is still true and young women who graduate from high school, college and university, work for a couple of years in a company before they get married. Once they marry, many leave the workforce to attend to domestic duties. As women are often excluded or discriminated against from promotion or responsibility in the office, they are less loyal or devoted to the companies than men. Married women might resume their jobs, but on a part-time basis. This makes part-time women less loyal to the company and they do not mind taking a long holiday to go abroad.

Although statistically more men travel abroad (due to business trips), the major market segments today are seniors (known as "Silver" groups), and middle-aged and the business travellers; followed by family groups and then young female office workers (known as OL for Office Ladies) (JATA, 2006). The main target twenty years ago was the Young Female Tourists, who were between the ages of 19 to 35, unmarried, and big spenders on souvenirs. They felt less obliged to buy souvenirs for their colleagues, and rather preferred to purchase expensive brand goods for themselves (Hashimoto, 1992; 2000). Now this group has grown into the middle-aged group. Women in their 30s and 50s are currently the most visible travelling groups (Personal communication, 2006b; c). The women in their 50s who were once the young office ladies, are now experienced and seasoned tourists. They are no longer as extravagant as before and they are not necessarily seeking to purchase expensive items (Personal communication, 2006b).

The Japanese are not a couple-oriented society. Husband and wife usually do not travel together until they reach retirement age. Husbands are busy working and cannot take a long holiday. Therefore, wives travel with their female friends or colleagues (Hashimoto, 1992; 2000). It is still applicable for wives in their 30s and 50s to travel without their husbands. Large numbers of women in their 40s are responsible for child rearing and they account for family travel during the summer holiday time, with or without husbands. The "Silver" groups are mostly of retired age and most of them are travelling as couples. This is the market segment that economic recession and recovery affects the least in their overseas holiday making, while demands of family and OL segments easily decline with economic conditions that show very slow recovery (JATA, 2006). The decision makers among the Silver groups and the middle-aged groups are usually the wives who already have some travel experience and tend to select the destinations or packages (Personal communication, 2006e).

6. Changing trends and information technology.

Historically, Japanese society has been considered to be an authoritarian society. It is still true that the opinion of the authority figure or teacher is highly valued. In terms of tourists' destination preferences, Japanese often consult travel guidebooks and magazines, which are known to set the trends. As Japanese have a totalitarian mentality, they do not want to be different from the rest of the group and tend to choose popular destinations that other people also visit. If an opinion leader mentions Europe for this year's destination, a large number of potential tourists will choose European destinations. Recent films such as the "Da Vinci Code" (France), Disney's Chronicles of Narnia: The Lion, The Witch and the Wardrobe (the UK), Harry Potter (the UK) in fact boosted tours to France and the UK (Personal communication, 2006e).

Although traditional media sources (TV and films, and print media) are still viewed as opinion leaders and the main source of influence, the spreading of information technology is changing travel trends among Japanese tourists. Telecommunication and information technology has changed access to travel products considerably. Incredibly, a small number of Japanese may have computers at home in comparison to North Americans, yet internet access and m-commerce (mobile commerce) is far more common in Japan by use of mobile phones. The leading travel magazine "a-broad" which introduces new travel products, popular destinations, and do's and don'ts of overseas traveling with lists of travel agents is now out of circulation after two decades in business. Time-constraint generations who can travel abroad tend to use internet services, e-commerce and m-commerce, and conventional intermediaries and information sources are becoming obsolete (Personal communication, 2006d). Young Japanese are more computer or technology literate and often do extensive search of information about tour price, places to visit and shops to go to. One source even believes that 40 per cent of the 60+ generation are familiar with the Internet (Ishihara, 2005). These computer savvy tourists do not wish to travel as a group and shop in the contracted shops of tour operators. As this group is very pragmatic, they tend to purchase skeleton packages (air tickets and accommodation, no fixed itinerary in the destination) to a fashionable destination. Some might hire a car in the destination and some might hop on local excursion tours (Personal communication, 2006b).

Canada as a Destination
In the specific case of Canada, the merger of national carriers Canadian Pacific Airlines and Air Canada eliminated competition and promotional deals, thereby losing attractiveness for Japanese intermediaries. With such a monopoly condition, the tour operators have limited attractive deals from healthy competition (Personal communication, 2006a). Canada is considered to be a long-haul destination. With additional security measures at airports in Canada or transit airports in the United States, there is a feeling it is spoiling the fun of holidaymaking. With a limited scope in destination

products for Japanese tourists, Canada is losing its attraction and with tedious and time-consuming travel procedures, it is losing its appeal (Personal communication, 2006a).

The main target segments for Canada are the "silver" groups who have already experienced various destinations, especially female tourists in this category. Although women in the 30s and 50s are a large active market, their destinations are currently focused on countries with heritage and history. This "silver" group demands "value for *my time*" which leads to the type of package tour in which the tourists will be satisfied with "well spent time" (Ishihara, 2005; JTB Grand Tours & Services, 2006a; b). Canada's main products have not changed for the past two decades or so: circuits of Vancouver, Banff, Toronto/Niagara Falls or Autumn Foliage tours of Ontario/Quebec. Unless these tourists have never visited Canada before, Canada cannot appeal to these lucrative and high demanding Japanese tourists.

Japanese society today is changing at an alarming rate. The most visible change is the social gap between the haves and have-nots. Polarized social classes are forming. Those who belong to the "haves" are capable of paying ¥ 570000 Economy class or ¥ 850000 Business class (CDN $ 5450 and $ 8100 respectively) per person for an eight day package "hiking" tour to Banff (JTB Grand Tours & Services, 2006c). The other group either do not travel overseas or look for short breaks: a 3-day package to Seoul, Korea can be as low as ¥ 25800 (CDN $250) (Hankyu Travel, 2006). Once the extravagant Young Female Japanese tourists, these ladies are now in their 40s and holding their purse strings tight and looking for alternative cheap destinations. These women are either too busy with child rearing with overworked husbands, or enjoying their single life and are making frequent short-haul tours with female friends. Economic recessions have profound psychological effects in the younger generation's mind. They are finding greater joy in smaller and inexpensive spending and less burdensome activities for recreation and pastimes. Recent corporate restructuring literally decimated the younger men's leisure-oriented life styles.

It is a challenge for Canada as a destination to create new products and a new image. If the Japanese market is the best spending target market, Canada has to conduct market research which not only shows demographics and the economic power of Japan as a nation but also social and psychological factors that are affecting current trends of outbound tourists. Canada as a destination projects an image of "natural beauty" and "wildlife" in the Japanese mind and this has not changed for over three decades. The Japanese market will not return if they have seen "the natural beauty" on their first visit to Canada. As long-haul destinations are losing their appeal to the Japanese market today, Canada as a destination needs to come up with variations of destinations, travel routes and activities which will be unique to Canada, and attractive to the repeat customers, with added value. For example, even though Canada is known for its natural environment, it has never fully tapped into the Japanese nature-loving characteristics. Hiking in Banff National Park is the latest product trying to appeal to Japanese nature lovers through walking in nature and discovering wild flowers. If Canada chooses to target the affluent "have" class of Japan, it does have much more to offer. For instance, Canada needs to market products such as the north, outdoor activities (both advanced and for novices), farming and fishing experiences, and camping with indigenous Canadians. Canada also has a rather short but rich history which is a great attraction to "heritage" loving Japanese. For example, the history of native Canadians, the migration of Europeans, the underground railway and the migration of Asians, especially the Japanese, are all products that may attract repeat customers. Canada has great resources and attractions, which are underutilized or not well matched to the needs of specific target markets.

CONCLUSION

Each destination has its own resources, attractions and varied tourism needs. Identifying what the destination can offer is as important as identifying the desirable target markets. However, to understand the target markets, conventional demographic and psychographic information is often not enough. Clearly understanding the social, cultural and psychological make-up of the target market will lead to a better knowledge of their motivations, expectations and requirements in the destination areas.This is not to suggest that destinations should change themselves in order to satisfy the desirable target markets; nonetheless, the destination can prepare to accommodate the special needs of the target markets, and to understand and tolerate or redirect peculiar behaviours of the target markets. If, for example, particular target markets never give tips or always try to bargain in shops, a good understanding of tourists' cultural and social background may explain the reasons for this and will enable local tourism businesses to handle such situations without offending the tourists, thus creating a more satisfying experience for the tourist and generating better business for local entrepreneurs.

As seen in the case of the Japanese as a target market, in over a decade, the society has changed, the economic situations have changed, and the psychology of holidaymaking has changed. The segment of female tourists who were once most spendthrifts has grown into the segment that has the tightest control over spending today. On the other hand, a new segment has emerged known as the "silver" group who are about to retire from work, are more affluent, more adventurous, and more eager to travel abroad as couples than other generations. Destinations will face the challenges of updating their target market profiles and keeping up with newly emerging target segments. If tourism is one of the most desired forms of regional or national development, destinations must find the way to optimise the benefits from tourism. It is crucial to target specific markets, to understand these markets more fully and to be aware that they can change quickly.

End Notes:
[1]This word was coined by the media in 1987. The word is a combi-nation of "Free" and "Arbeiter", a German word for worker. Arbeitier, however, is commonly used as a "part-time worker" in Japanese. However, Freeters are differentiated from the part-time labour force due to the fact that part-time workers are expect to fill in the gap of the regular work force, assume uncompensated long overworked hours and receive little or no benefits from the work place.

REFERENCES

BBC (2005) "Japan women's singular contentment", BBC NEWS retrieved from http://newsvote.bbc.co.uk/mpapps/pagetools/print/news.bbc.co.uk/2/hi/asia-pacific/4296877.stm

BBC (2006) "Japanese land prices bounce back", retrieved from http://news.bbc.co.uk/2/hi/business/5234478.stm

Canadian Tourism Commission (2000a) *Japan-Canada two-way tourism current situation, Appendix to Summary of Proceedings: 7th Canada-Japan Tourism Conference, April 26-28, 2000, Ottawa, Ontario, Canada*, Ottawa: Canadian Tourism Commission.

Canadian Tourism Commission (2000b) *Summary of Proceedings: 7th Canada-Japan Tourism Conference, April 26-28, 2000, Ottawa, Ontario, Canada*, Ottawa: Canadian Tourism Commission.

Canadian Tourism Commission. (2000c) *1999 Tourism Highlights* (leaflet), Ottawa: Canadian Tourism Commission.

Canadian Tourism Commission (2004) Annual Report 2003: Collective Efforts, Common Goals, retrieved from http://origin.www.canadatourism.com/ctx/files/publication/data/en_ca/general_publications/annual_report_2003/AR%202003%20EN.pdf

Canadian Tourism Commission (2005) Annual Report 2004: The Power of Attraction, retrieved from http://origin.www.canadatourism.com/ctx/files/publication/data/en_ca/general_publications/annual_report_2004/AR%202004%20EN.pdf

Canadian Tourism Commission (2006) Annual Report 2005: Explorations, retrieved from http://www.canadatourism.com/ctx/files/publication/data/en_ca/general_publications/2005/annual_report/Annual_Report_01-05-06-en_web.pdf

CTC (2004) "Banff Set to host 2004 Canada-Japan Tourism Conference", Canada Touirsm.com Press Releases, retrieved from http://origin.www.canadatourism.com/ctx/app/en/ca/pressItem.do?articleId=53127&language=english

Hamilton-Oehrl, A. (1998) "Leisure Parks in Japan", in Linhart, S. and Frühstück, S. (eds.), *The Culture of Japan as Seen Through its Leisure*, New York: State University of New York Press, 237-250.

Hankyu Travel (2006) e-very Super Free de Seoul 3 days, retrieved from http://ec.hankyu-travel.com/hei/vsheitour/WEB/hei_tour3_tour.aspx?p_company_cd=1000014&p_course_no=00002233&p_date=&p_naigai=W&p_hatsu=001&p_user_com=&p_baitai=&p_disp=2

Hashimoto, A. (1992) *A Socio-Psychological Approach to the Consumer Behaviour of Young Female Japanese Tourists*, Unpublished Masters (MSc) dissertation, University of Surrey,

Guildford (Surrey) UK.

Hashimoto, A. (2000) "Young Japanese female tourists: an in-depth understanding of a market segment", *Current Issues in Tourism*, 3(1):35-50.

Ishihara, Y. (2005) "JTB gurando tsuah and sahbisu no chosen" [Challenge of JTB Grand Tours and Services], Choryu – Unjou Kaisei, retrieved from http://jwing.exblog.jp/m2005-07-01/#3249677

JATA (2006) Dai 17 kai JATA Ryokou-shijou Doukou Chousa – Kaigai (2006-nen 6-gatuki) [The 17th Travel Market Movement Survey – Overseas (June 2006)] retrieved from http://www.jata-net.or.jp/tokei/shijo/060628/01.htm

JTB Grand Tours & Services (2006a) Concept, retrieved from http://www.jtb-grandtours.jp/concept/greetings.html

JTB Grand Tours & Services (2006b) Sales Point, retrieved from http://www.jtb-grandtours.jp/salespoint/salespoint_03.html

JTB Grand Tours & Services, (2006c) Canadian Rockies Natural Walk 8 Days, retrieved from http://www.jgts.jp/tour/1163/1163.html

Koumelis, T. (2006) "Delegates of the Canadian Tourism Commission (CTC) speak to the Canada-Japan Tourism Conference", TDN International Edition Daily Travel & Tourism Newsletter, retrieved from http://www.Traveldialynews.com/news_print.asp?newID=27387

McCurry, J. (2006) "Japan to tell its workers: take time off - for the sake of the nation", The Guardian, retrieved from http://www.guardian.co.uk/japan/story/0,7369,1687925,00.ht

ml

MLIT (2006a) Heisei 17 nendo kankou no joukyou [2005 Tourism Activities], retrieved from www.mlit.go.jp/hakusho/kankou-hakusho/h18/images/01.pdf

MLIT (2006b) Heisei 18 nendo kankou seisaku [2006 Tourism Policy], retrieved from www.mlit.go.jp/hakusho/kankou-hakusho/h18/images/02.pdf

Nitta, H (2006) "Capitalizing on Retirement of Japan's First Baby-Boomers", JETRO Japan Economic Report, April-May 2006, retrieved from www.jetro.go.jp/en/market/trend/special/pdf/jem0605-1e.pdf

Okubo, M. (2005) "Summer holidays!" Child Research Net, retrieved from http://www.childresearch.net/PROJECT/YRP/2005/PAPER12.HTM

Smith, S.L.J. (1995) *Tourism Analysis: A Handbook*, (Second Edition), Harlow, UK: Longman.

Statistics Canada (2003) Canadian Tourism Facts & Figures 2002, retrieved from http://origin.www.canadatourism.com/ctx/files/Research_Files/F_F_Brochure2002.pdf

Statistics Canada (2004) Canadian Tourism Facts & Figures 2003, retrieved from http://origin.www.canadatourism.com/ctx/files/Research_Files/F_F_Brochure2003_E.pdf

Statistics Canada (2005) Canadian Tourism Facts & Figures 2004, retrieved from http://origin.www.canadatourism.com/ctx/files/Research_Files/F_F_Brochure2004_E.pdf

Telfer, D. and Hashimoto, A. (2000) "Niagara Icewine Tourism: Japanese Souvenir Purchases at Inniskillin Winery", *Tourism and Hospitality Research: The Surrey Quarterly Review*, 2(4): 343-354.

The Canadian Trade Commissioner Service (2006) Canada-Japan Relations: Overview (Last Updated: 2006/07/15), retrieved fromhttp://www.infoexport.gc.ca/ie-en/DisplayDocument.jsp? did=845

Tourism Staff (2006) "Canada - Japan Tourism Conference 2006", CanadaTouirsm.com News& Events, retrieved from http://origin.www.canadatourism.com/ctx/app/en/ca/newsItem.do?articleId=62418&language=english

Tourism Staff (2006) "Building for the future: Canada - Japan conference results", Tourism Magazine, .003(07) retrieved from http://origin.www.canadatourism.com/ctx/app/en/ca/magazine/article.do?path=templatedata%5Cctx%5CmagArticle%5Cdata%5Cen%5C2006%5Cissue02%5Cmarketing%5Ccanada_japan

Web Japan (2005) "Time to Retire", Trends in Japan retrieved from http://web-japan.org/trends/business/bus050812.html

Wiseman, P. (2004) "No sex please – we're Japanese", USA TODAY, retrieved from http://www.usatoday.com/news/world/2004-06-02-japan-women-usat_x.htm

9

The Internet and Tourism

Lorri Krebs

INTRODUCTION

The Internet has been adopted in society in many forms, such as a communication device, an information source, a social activity and an educative tool. Almost since its inception, the Internet has also been inextricably linked to economics, creating the demand for new products and services. Methods of conducting business have evolved with new opportunities for marketing, sales, purchasing and performing transactions. The Internet has been embraced by many economic sectors and the tourism industry is no exception. However, many smaller tourism businesses are reluctant to invest significant resources into this "on-line phenomenon". These smaller "mom and pop" types of businesses comprise the majority of tourism endeavours and, in many cases, the operators do not have the knowledge or understanding of the Internet to make informed decisions about how to use it within their businesses. Obtaining answers to questions such as "Are certain types of tourists more inclined to use the Internet?" and "Can tourists be segmented into specific markets according to Internet use?" may clarify the extent to which the Internet has been adopted by tourists and alleviate some of the concerns of these small business owners. However, it is also important to provide an historic platform to see where the Internet came from and why it has been adopted so readily by tourists.

A wide variety of research has been published on the Internet and tourism yet, for many users and suppliers, the primary concern is booking or reserving tickets on-line. This chapter will explore the various links that exist among the Internet and tourism, provide an historical context, discuss some of the important issues concerning the role of the Internet in decision making and conclude with some ideas concerning balancing supply and demand in the context of the continually changing Internet usage patterns.

THE INTERNET AS A MARKETING TOOL IN TOURISM

The first established relationship between the Internet and tourism was probably the use of the Internet as a marketing tool. As such, we will begin by exploring the various connections within this context. When the marketing of any product or service is examined, quite often we begin by looking at the effectiveness of the advertisement or the media through which the ad is being presented to the consumer. Tourism is certainly no different in these respects. The impacts on decision making are important in determining what products will be purchased or used and which destination(s) will be visited. In fact, there are few Internet users who can not say that they have not been bothered by banners or pop-ups through which trips or destinations are being sold. As Marshall McLuhan (1962) stated "the medium is the message", so perhaps it is the media that may have as much influence as the ad itself. Keeping this in mind, we will briefly explore a history of tourism marketing.

Historically, how did people first find out about where to travel or why they might want to go? Probably word of mouth – before the written word, people might have suggested that a particular place was attractive, tranquil or had great healing powers, or that there was a religious incentive to go somewhere and the 'somewhere' was determined by listening to others' personal experiences. But regardless of why one engages in travel, the destination would probably have been chosen through a recommendation from another person. Word of mouth, or referrals from friends or family, is still one of the most important inputs into tourism decision making. In fact, Um and Crompton (1990) found that social stimuli, mostly the recommendations of friends and relatives, dominate today as the most important information source in travel decision making.

Another historic motivator to travel may have been from reading tales in books, such as *Ulysses* in the *Odyssey* (one of the great ancient 'tourism' novels), the *Canterbury Tales* or, in more recent times, Joseph Conrad's the *Heart of Darkness*. All of these books discuss travel and may have influenced travel patterns in the past. Today, however, we often see guidebooks as motivators for certain travel products.

Another motivator to travel came in the form of newspaper and magazine advertisements. In the mid 1800s, newspaper ads began to market travel and these, in turn, begat flyers and posters. More recently, our newspapers have incorporated actual travel sections with stories and advertisements designed to act as referrals from trusted sources in the hope that potential tourists will react in their decision making with the same confidence as they would to a personal referral from a friend. The *New Yorker* or *Harper's Review* may have been among the first magazines to advertise travel, but today there are magazines, *National Geographic Traveler and Condé Nast*, that not only advertise but also focus their stories on tourism destinations.

Newspapers and magazines were soon followed by the invention of radio and, close on its heels, the television. Ads, travel shows, destinations and specific pursuits shown on TV shows have all heavily influenced travel patterns (Litman, 1982). The television "is set apart from competing media by its ability to offer sight, sound and motion to generate an emotional response" (TVB, 2005:1). By using the qualities of television (sight, sound and motion), advertisers could generate trust, emotion and excitement that could not have been created as well through any other medium until that point. Simply put, people enjoy television and that is why it is so widely adopted and so frequently used. The pursuits shown on TV have had and still have an enormous influence on decision making in tourism.

Similar to the impacts of TV on tourism marketing, Travel Agents have also had an undeniable influence in tourism decision making. However, the Internet encompasses all of the same qualities of the aforementioned marketing tools. As examples:

- Current day blogs can be equated to the impacts of story telling from the past – personal referrals and accounts of travel.
- One can compare prices of travel similar to the newspaper ads, looking for the 'best' published deal.
- Standard advertisements now come in the form of unsolicited e-mail, pop-ups or banner ads on Web sites.
- Travel agents are available on the Internet.

In addition, computers offer some of the same qualities as television - sound, sight and motion – and, therefore, many of the same responses can be generated from users such as trust, emotion and excitement. Just as the effects on decision making from TV viewing has been shown as being a powerful force, with similar qualities being found in Internet use, one can speculate that the Internet could have the same perceived authority in current marketing and decision making. Before exploring the marketing-Internet-tourism connections further, a brief history of the Internet will be provided as background to the discussion. This will include a consideration of how the innovation is adopted within society and an examination of current Internet use patterns within tourism.

HISTORY OF THE INTERNET

The United States formed a special agency within the Department of Defence known as the Advanced Research Projects Agency (ARPA). ARPA was responsible for establishing an American lead in science and technology, which would be applicable to the military. One of its first recommendations was the development of a reliable communications network that could withstand massive destruction. According to the original directors of ARPA however, the well-circulated story that the Internet was developed for use in the event of a nuclear holocaust is incorrect (Leiner *et al.*, 1987). In 1969, ARPA's communications network was established and was able to link the military with four universities: the University of California at Los Angeles, Stanford University, the University of California at Santa Barbara and the University of Utah. The network was called ARPANET and was designed to be used primarily for research purposes. Within two years, ARPANET hosted, or connected, 23 universities and government research centres on an international scale. In 1971, electronic mail, or email, was invented although it was not until 1988 that Internet Relay Chat (IRC) was created and provided the first forum for real-time communication. In 1989 Gopher, a very basic Internet interface, was created and allowed users to subscribe to newsgroups as a primary method of information exchange. This very basic interface was the beginning of the Internet as we know it today. Three years later in 1992, CERN released the World Wide Web, the huge virtual hypertext network which most people use to surf the Net.

Leiner *et al.* (1997) summarized the history of the Internet and found that it there are four distinct patterns that mirror how society adopts innovations (see Rogers, 1962 and 1986). In the beginning, a technological evolution occurs and, in the case of the Internet, that began with early research on packet switching and the ARPANET (and related technologies). Ongoing research continues "to expand the horizons of the infrastructure along several dimensions, such as scale, performance, and higher level functionality" (Leiner *et al.*, 1997:1). The second focus or pattern is often on the operations and management aspects of the infrastructure needed for such a complex system on a grander scale; in the case of the Internet, the global level. The social aspect of a new innovation is the third concern and, in the past, this has been the impetus to have various systems work together to create and evolve the technology. The fourth pattern surrounds the commercialization aspect and, for the Internet, has resulted "in an extremely effective transition of research results

into a broadly deployed and available information infrastructure"
(Leiner *et al.*, 1997:2).

ADOPTION OF INNOVATION IN SOCIETY

To understand how innovation behaviour becomes established, marketers usually consult the diffusion of innovations model developed
by Everett Rogers (1962). According to this widely used theory, certain types of easily identifiable people are predicted to embrace
innovations at specific times and in patterned ways.

The initial innovators tend to be young, upscale, educated people who know what they want. These are generally the first to
embrace any new product, service or channel of distribution. The
second market segment, called the early adopters by Rogers (1962),
exhibits many of the same characteristics as the initial group but is
not seen as being a group of risk takers. These are followed by the
early majority and, finally, the late majority of society.

The Rogers model predicts that various market segments learn
about products from the groups that are adjacent to them in terms of
social class. However, in the case of the Internet these patterns did
not emerge. The initial adopters were consistent with the theory in
terms of social class, education and various other demographics.
However, atypical groups followed. The 'hackers' were the next
large group within society to rapidly embrace the Internet. Hackers,
although typically young, did not necessarily reflect the demographic criteria usually attributed to the early adopters. They were
neither particularly highly educated nor in the higher income brack-
ets. They gained computer skills and access in spite of the fact that
they emerged from a variety of social classes. The third group to
rapidly adopt the Internet was the 'grassroots' market segment who
utilized computer skills to lead more effective lives. The 'grassroots' were typically middle-aged or retired people who are normally associated with the late majority group. In the case of the
Internet, this group led the early majority. The late majority are still

seeking a reason to 'join in', frequently citing financial concerns or difficulties in understanding the technology as barriers to adoption.

Statistics on the actual numbers of global Internet users should be viewed with caution. The reliability of the information depends on how and why the source collected the data. If figures from a variety of sources are compared, the differences in the estimates range across millions of users. However, it can be comfortably reported that Europe and Asia currently have the fastest growing on-line populations. In comparison, North America has seen little or no recent growth in its on-line population suggesting that this market may be reaching a saturation point. In 2003, Google, the most widely accessed North American search engine, quoted the following statistics on numbers of users:

World Total Internet Users 605.60 million
- Africa 6.31 million
- Asia/Pacific 187.24 million
- Europe 190.91 million
- Middle East 5.12 million
- Canada and USA 182.67 million
- Latin America 33.35 million

Depending on the source, many different numbers are promulgated. An Internet company such as Google or Yahoo may inflate numbers to try and to gain the confidence of users and encourage advertisers to join them. A different advertising medium, such as a magazine company, may quote lower numbers of Internet users to try to retain their own market share of advertisers.

Information on the historical evolution of the Internet and statistics on the number of Internet users, while indicating recent growth and massive size, in themselves do not shed much light on the role of the Internet in tourism. Thus it is necessary to understand in what **capacity** the Internet is being used by potential and actual tourists. A two-year study, which surveyed 1,209 tourists during various travel stages, and explored their Internet use patterns throughout these stages, will be discussed in more detail in the following sections as the current role of the Internet in tourism is examined.

EXPLORING THE INTERNET IN TOURISM

Tourism research has traditionally focused on either the supply or the demand side, with the majority of academic studies investigating the demand side (Aroch, 1985; Crouch, 1994; Lee, 1996; Klaric, 1999; McCabe, 2000). Recently however, there has been a call for a more integrated approach to tourism research (Jamal and Hollinshead, 2001). Conceivably, looking at both sides at the same time will allow a more balanced understanding of particular issues to be achieved. For example, the use of the Internet in tourism depends on the fact that suppliers have an on-line presence. It would be impossible to examine how the Internet influences decisions in tourism if there were not a supply for people to look for and access. In addition, it would be insufficient to examine the supply (presence of suppliers on the Internet) without also considering the demand (Internet user) for information. Thus, it is important to explore both the supply and demand, and to investigate the Internet as a link between the two. To what extent does the Internet provide this link and how important is it for potential and actual tourists? Figure 9.1 provides examples of the various connections that can be explored within the context of the Internet and tourism.

As mentioned earlier, when examining the effectiveness of marketing tools, what is really being sought is an assessment of the impacts of the various information sources on decision making. Did a particular advertisement, book or experience, for example, influence decisions? Baloglu (2000) suggested that the evaluation of tourism destinations is determined by the amount of information available, the types of information sources used and socio-psychological travel motivations. The variety of information sources used was found to be a strong predictor of image. The types of information sources had different effects on the images of destinations' offerings. For example, word-of-mouth information influenced perceptions of the quality of experience, while advertisements influenced perceptions of value and / or the environment. Non-promotional sources, such as books and movies, influenced perceptions of destination attractiveness. Baloglu (2000:85) concluded that "different types of information sources have varying degrees of effects on perceptual and cognitive evaluation".

Supply	Intermediaries
- Web site design	- Travel agents
- Advertising	- Web browsers
- Destination Marketing Organizations	- Local government
- Hotels, restaurants	• Economic development opportunities
- Airlines	- National level
- Car rental	• Marketing Canada
	• Communicating within Canada
Demand	(for example Canadian Tourism
- Number of users	Commission)
- Demographics	
- Socio-cultural	
- How often	**Academic**
- Clicking behaviour	- Patterns of adoption
- Attractiveness	- Patterns of use
- Efficiency	- Patterns of communication
- Satisfaction	- Patterns of travel
	- Economics
Virtual Tourism	- Using the Internet as a research method
	- Teaching tourism on the Internet

Figure 9.1: Tourism and Internet Use Examples.

Other studies have examined information sources in terms of factors influencing travel behaviour intentions and destination choice (Court and Lupton, 1997; Vogt and Fesenmaier, 1998). Mayo and Jarvis (1981) modeled travel decision making and proposed that information sources form beliefs and opinions about a destination, thus creating an image of that destination.

Image formation has been widely studied in motivational and decision-making research (Dilley, 1986; Cohen, 1993; Gartner, 1993; Dann, 1996; Lubbe, 1998; Baloglu, 2000). Images have been shown to result from a variety of stimuli which are connected to information sources (Woodside and Lysonski, 1989). Woodside and Lysonski's (1989) model of traveler destination choice emphasized tourism information sources as significant determinants of destination images. Much of the current research on information searches by potential and actual tourists has focused either on a particular place or one particular type of tourist or activity. For example, Hyde (2000) found that for international travelers to New Zealand, the majority of information search and planning occurred only after arrival in the country. Detailed plans had usually only been arranged for the first 24 hours of the holiday during pre-trip planning. In contrast, Milner (2000) found that Japanese travelers to Alaska conducted the majority of their information searches prior to travel and had purchased most of their tour product prior to their arrival.

In this context then, it is necessary to explore the role of the Internet in such decisions and to enquire at what stage of travel people are accessing the Internet for information. Recent studies have been published which indicate that certain information sources are more important at certain stages of travel. For example, many TV commercials target people who have no intention to travel at the time but try to induce them to choose their destination when the time comes. My own studies show that people search the Internet during all of the travel stages, but to a different extent and in search of different types of information.

Modeled after MacKay and Fesenmaier (1998), travel can be broken down into five stages: 1) no intention of taking a trip; 2) preplanning a trip; 3) finalizing a trip; 4) purchasing a trip; and 5) actually on the trip. If we look at general Internet use over the five stages of travel, we find the pattern shown in Figure 9.2.

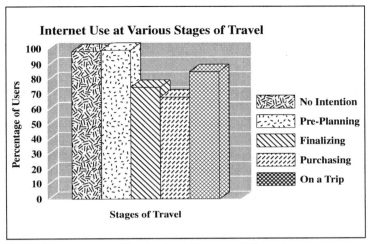

Figure 9.2: Internet Use during 5 Stages of Travel.

It shows that potential and actual tourists do in fact access the Internet in all stages of travel but to varying degrees. All of the people surveyed who utilized the Internet, had used the Internet during the pre-planning stage of their travels. Yet only 68.3 per cent indicated use of the Internet to purchase travel or travel-related products. Slightly more respondents felt comfortable enough to make reservations (75.2 per cent) but they were reluctant to perform monetary transactions using the Internet. While the respondents were actually on the trip, many (86.1 per cent) indicated that they consult the Internet for information on activities and further planning, reserving and booking.

One of the major factors that influence a consumer's decision to purchase a product or service is information (Andereck and Caldwell, 1993). The information or awareness that a person already has about a product or service, in addition to the information that they are able to gather and the credibility of such information, are all critical to the consumer in a decision to purchase (Raitz and Dakhil, 1989). In tourism, the availability of information is particularly significant as the consumers are commonly located at some distance from the desired product or service (Wicks and Schuett, 1991).

Information searches are particularly important to tourists because much tourism has the following characteristics:

1)   a trip involves using discretionary money and free time, and is a high risk purchase;
2)   the intangible nature of services suggests that secondary or tertiary sources must be used for information as a consumer is not able actually to observe the potential product or service to be purchased;
3)   vacationers are often interested in visiting new, unfamiliar destinations as a primary travel motive (Gitelson and Crompton, 1983).

Information search behaviour may also partly depend on consumer preferences for specific information sources (Andereck and Caldwell, 1993). For example, in 1994, 66 per cent of those seeking tour packages were strongly influenced by travel agent recommendations (Tourism Canada, 1994). However, since that time, the role of the travel agent has tended to decline as fewer airlines compensate the agents for their work and the Internet has become an increasingly important and convenient service provider. Harris and Brown (1992) also examined information sources used by travelers. Their demographic analyses indicated that certain segments of the population prefer to use particular information sources.

The author's own study of the Internet and tourism (Ref.) showed that different types of information were looked for on the Internet depending on the stage of travel. Eight types of information are sought:

1)   General information about a destination
2)   Accommodation

3) Attractions
4) Transportation
5) Events
6) Cultural features
7) Web site links
8) Categories of types of travel

A summary of the types of information and their overall relative importance to the respondents is found in Figure 9.3. However, the different types of information also obviously became more or less important depending on the stage of travel the respondents were in.

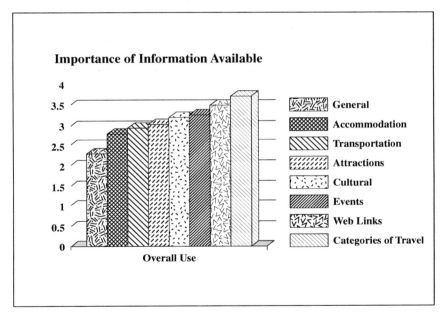

Figure 9.3: Importance of Information

The respondents were asked to rate the importance of each type of information at the various stages. On a scale of 1 to 7, with 1 being the most important, and 7 being the least important, all types of information rated as being somewhat important for people to access with general information on destinations and activities considered to be the most important to them at all travel stages.

Having looked briefly at how and why tourists are using the Internet, attention will now be turned to the supply side. So what is the supplier's role and why do we need to look at supply at all? One obvious answer is that there needs to be a Web site for users to be able to access. Marketing implies that a supplier is marketing or advertising *to* or *for* a certain target group or market. In order to do this, they need to know why they want to use the Internet as part of their marketing strategy. This may sound simple enough but, when suppliers are asked this question, they often cannot provide an answer. In response to the author's surveys, most of the businesses, especially the smaller or newer ones, felt that they needed an Internet presence but it was perceived as being too expensive to have a Web site designed and many felt that they did not understand it sufficiently and so they were reluctant to become involved. Of the many suppliers interviewed for this research, only one supplier who had a Web site had actually thought carefully about what they hoped to gain from their Internet presence. Interestingly, their prime purpose for having a web site was to avoid direct contact with visitors. The intention was that the site would be used for information only and to provide links to members' (local businesses) sites as well as to other information that tourists may want. In fact, if someone does contact this particular supplier with a question, they will subsequently update the Web site to include the information so that they will not get any more identical questions.

Many tourists that were surveyed, who were all Internet users, indicated that they wanted a site that would allow them to check availability, make reservations and accept payment and just over half indicated that they perform monetary transactions over the Internet (engage in e-commerce). However, in the end, suppliers really control use – if it is not there, people cannot use it. As such, it is extremely difficult to gauge the actual effectiveness of the Internet as a marketing tool. What the respondents in this study wanted from the Internet was not always what was available and their final decisions reflected this.

It can be concluded at this point that, from an advertising and marketing perspective, if a supplier wants to increase market share then the Internet should probably be included and budgeted for in their marketing plans. Neglecting the Internet as an advertising tool ensures that a certain percentage of potential tourists will NOT visit nor will they use their tourism product or service.

The second pattern that was noticed is that when a property has no presence on the Internet, the tourists and potential tourists will not patronize but go elsewhere, regardless of their original intention. In the final analysis, it did not matter what was recommended to them by their friends or relatives (usually the biggest determinant in decision making) if they could not book it on-line. Therefore, the answer to the question "Is the Internet an effective marketing tool in tourism?", the answer is "Yes", but only to the extent that people are using it. The Internet can not lure a 'new' market segment. Also, if suppliers want to maintain their existing market segment; they should be prepared to invest in their Web sites.

When attempting to relate Internet use to market segments or typologies, it is apparent that it may be necessary to re-examine the demographics of tourists themselves. Do the original typologies that were presented in the literature still hold true? Second, Internet use in tourism is often linked primarily to wealthy tourists yet the Internet is a product of the computer and its use will continue to change. More questions continue to arise, perhaps more than the answers that can be provided, such as "How will the process of change and evolution itself be managed?" As a society we do not lack vision, motivation or the ability to evolve technologically, but can we collectively set a direction for the future that allows us to continue to develop tourism-related strategies as information technology continues to grow and change?

CONCLUSIONS

Throughout this chapter, the Internet has been viewed as a marketing tool that is employed in various aspects of tourism. The Internet has been shown to have the capability to be more than a simple medium through which travel can be advertised; however many tourism operators lack the skills or knowledge to use the Internet to match the users' demands effectively. A brief history of how the Internet has been adopted within society was provided as the context for a discussion of Internet use patterns. Areas where there are gaps between supply and demand were emphasized.

One of the key links between the Internet and tourism was shown to be the impacts on decision making. Consumer preferences for certain types of media, such as recommendations of friends or TV advertisements, that may inadvertently sway a tourist to choose one product over another have been important historically to decision making. However, the Internet has been shown to encompass many of the same qualities and characteristics found in these alternative media, thereby having a stronger influence than any one particular medium on its own.

Patterns of Internet use revealed that for consumers who use the Internet, if a particular tourism-related product is not available on the Internet, they will be less likely to purchase that product. Suppliers then should perhaps re-examine their marketing strategies to ensure that they have some presence on the Internet. Even a simple link and basic Web page will ensure that a potential customer will, at the very least, include the product among their potential choices.

The connections between the Internet and tourism have been explored in many contexts and while the number of Internet users seems to have reached a plateau in terms of growth, *how* people are utilizing the Internet continues to change and new technologies are being embraced. However, the foundations for decision making in tourism seem to change at a much slower rate and often the 'tried and true' prevails. In the final analysis, the Internet will continue to be important to tourism as more than a simple marketing tool and to society as more than just the newest technological advancement.

REFERENCES

Andereck, K.L. and Caldwell, L.L. (1993) "The Influence of tourists' characteristics on ratings of information sources for an attraction", *Journal of Travel and Tourism Marketing*, 2(2/3): 171-189.

Aroch, R. (1985) "Socio-economic research into tourist motivation and demand patterns", *Tourist Review*, 40(4): 27-29.

Baloglu, S. (2000) "A path-analytical model of visitation intention involving information sources, socio-psychological motivations and destination images", in A. G. Woodside, G. I. Crouch, J. A. Mazanec, M. Oppermann and M. Y. Sakai (eds.), *Consumer Psychology of Tourism, Hospitality and Leisure*, Wallingford, UK: CABI, 63-90.

Baloglu, S. and McCleary, K.W. (1999) "A model of destination image formation", *Annals of Tourism Research*, 868-897.

Cohen, E. (1993) "The study of touristic images of native people: mitigating the stereotype of a stereotype", in D.G. Pearce and R.W. Butler (eds.), *Tourism Research: Critiques and Challenges*, London: Routledge, 36-69.

Court, B. and Lupton, R.A. (1997) "Customer portfolio development: modelling destination adopters, inactives and rejectors", *Journal of Travel Research*, 36: 35-43.

Crouch, G.I. (1994) "Promotion and demand in international tourism", in J.C. Crotts and W.F. van Raaij (eds.), *Economic Psychology of Travel and Tourism*, New York: Haworth Press Inc., 109-125.

CyberAtlas.com (2001) Marketing on the Internet, CyberAtlas. Internet.com.

Dann, G.M.S. (1996) "Tourist images of a destination - an alternative analysis, in D.R. Fesenmaier, J.T. O'Leary and M. Uysal (eds.), *Recent Advances in Tourism Marketing Research*, New York: Hayworth Press, 41-55.

Dilley, R.S. (1986) "Tourist brochures and tourist images", *The Canadian Geographer*, 30(1): 59-65.

Gartner, W. (1993) "Image Formation Process", *Journal of Travel and Tourism Marketing*, 2(2/3): 191-225.

Gitelson, R. and Crompton, J.L. (1983) "The planning horizons and sources of information used by pleasure vacationers", *Journal of Travel Research*, 22: 2-7.

Harris, C.C. and Brown, G. (1992) "Gain, loss and personal responsibility: the role of motivation in resource valuation decision-making", *Ecological Economics*, 5(1): 73-92.

Hyde, K.F. (2000) "A hedonic perspective on independent vacation planning, decision making and behaviour", in A.G. Woodside, G.I. Crouch, J.A. Mazanec, M. Oppermann and M.Y. Sakai (eds.), *Consumer Psychology of Tourism, Hospitality and Leisure*, Wallingford, UK: CABI, 177-191.

Jamal, T. and Hollinshead, K. (2001) "Tourism and the forbidden zone: the underserved power of qualitative inquiry", *Tourism*

Management, 22: 63-82.

Klaric, Z. (1999) "Impact of distance and availability of information on travel to conflict regions - example of Croatia", *Turizam*, 47(1): 26-35.

Kotler, P., Haider, H.D. and Rein, I. (1993) *Marketing Places*, New York: The Free Press.

Lee, C.K. (1996) "Major determinants of international tourism demand for South Korea: inclusion of marketing variable", *Journal of Travel and Tourism Marketing*, 5(1/2): 101-111.

Lee, T.-H. and Crompton, J.L. (1992) "Measuring novelty seeking in tourism", *Annals of Tourism Research*, 19: 732-751.

Litman, B. (1982) "Decision making in the film industry: the influence of the TV market", *Journal of Communication*, 21(3): 33.

Leiner, B.M., Cerf, V., Clark, D., Kahn, R., Kleinrock, L., Lynch, D., Postel, D., Roberts, L, and Wolff, S. (1997) A Brief History of the Internet, Part I, http://www.isoc.org/oti/articles/0597/leiner.html

Lubbe, B. (1998) "Primary image as a dimension of destination image: an empirical assessment", *Journal of Travel and Tourism Marketing*, 7(4): 21-43.

MacKay, K.J. and Fesenmaier, D.R. (1998) "A process approach to segmenting the getaway travel market", *Journal of Travel and Tourism Marketing*, 7(3): 1-18.

Mathieson, A. and Wall, G. (1982) *Tourism: Economic, Social and Physical Impacts*, London: Longman.

Mayo, E.J. and Jarvis, L.P. (1981) *The Psychology of Leisure Travel*, Boston: CDI Publishing.

Mazanec, J.A. (1995) "Constructing traveller types", in B. Butler and D.G. Pearce (eds.), *Change in Tourism, People, Places, Processes*, London: Routledge.

McCabe, S. (2000) "The problem of motivation in understanding the demand for leisure day visits", in A.G. Woodside, G.I. Crouch, J.A. Mazanec, M. Oppermann and M.Y. Sakai (eds.), *Consumer Psychology of Tourism, Hospitality and Leisure*, Wallingford: CABI Publishing, 211-226.

McLuhan, M. (1962) *The Guttenberg Galaxy*, Toronto: University of Toronto Press.

_____ (1964) *Understanding Media: The Extensions of Man*, New York: McGraw-Hill.

McLuhan, M. and Powers, B.R. (1989) *The Global Village, Transformations in World Life and Media in the 21st Century*, New York: Oxford University Press.

Milner, L.M., Collins, J.M., Tachibana, R. and Hiser, R. (2000) "The Japenese vacation visitor to Alaska: a preliminary examination of peak and off season traveler demographics, information source utilization, trip planning, and customer satisfaction", *Journal of Travel and Tourism Marketing*, 9(1/2): 43-56.

Raitz, K. and Dakhil, M. (1989) "A note about information sources for preferred recreational environments", *Journal of Travel Research*, 30: 45-49.

Tourism Canada (1994) *Product Distribution in the Tourism Industry: A Profile of Tour Operators and Travel Agencies in*

Canada, Ottawa: Supply and Services Canada.

TVB Television Bureau of Canada (2005) Television Basics, http://www.tvb.ca/tvbasics.pdf

Um, S. and Crompton, J.L. (1990) "Attitude determinants in tourism destination choice", *Annals of Tourism Research*, 17: 432-448.

Vogt, C.A. and Fesenmaier, D.R. (1998) "Expanding the functional information search model", *Annals of Tourism Research*, 25(3): 551-578.

Vogt, C.A. and Andereck, K. (2003) "Destination perceptions across a vacation", *Journal of Travel Research*, 41: 348-355.

Wicks, B.E. and Schuett, M.A. (1991) "Examining the role of tourism promotion through the use of brochures", *Tourism Management*, 11: 301-312.

Woodside, A.G. and Lysonski, S. (1989) "A general model of travel destination choice", *Journal of Travel Research*, 27: 8-14.

List of Contributors

Stephen Smith
Department of Recreation and Leisure Studies
University of Waterloo

Noga Collins-Kreiner
University of Haifa

Geoff McBoyle
Geography Department
University of Waterloo

Sanjay K. Nepal
Recreation, Park and Tourism Sciences
Texas A & M University

David Weaver
School of Hotel, Restaurant and Tourism Management
University of South Carolina

John Tunbridge
Carleton University

Brian S. Osborne
Queen's University

Atsuko Hashimoto
Department of Tourism and Environment
Brock University

Lorri Krebs
Geography Department
Salem State College

University of Waterloo

Department of Geography Publication Series

Available from:
Geography Publications   Phone: 519-888-4567; Ext. 3278
University of Waterloo   Fax: 519-746-0658
Waterloo, Ontario, Canada   e-mail: bkevans@fes.uwaterloo.ca
N2L 3G1

http://www.fes.uwaterloo.ca/Research/GeogPubs/geogpub.html

Series

62 Cabana, R. and Wagner, F. (2006) *The International Faces of Urban Sprawl: A Study of Six Metropolitan Regions in North America*, ISBN 0-921083-73-4, 314 pages.

61 Wismer, S., Babcock, T. and Nurkin, B. (2005) *From Sky to Sea: Environment and Development in Sulawesi*, ISBN 0-921083-72-6, 708 pages.

60 Shrubsole, D. and Watson, N. (2005) *Sustaining Our Futures: Reflections on Environment, Economy and Society*, ISBN 0-921083-71-8, 602 pages.

59 Gertler, L.O. (2005) *Radical Rumblings: Confessions of a Peripatetic Planner*, ISBN 0-921083-70-X, 330 pages.

58 Sanderson, Marie (2004) *Weather and Climate in Southern Ontario*, ISBN 0-921083-69-6, 138 pages.

57 Behmel, Friedrich P. (2004) *International Development Assistance Work Focused on Tropical Smallholder Families: Learning Through Trial and Error*, ISBN 0-921083-68-8, 270 pages.

56 Theberge, J.B. and Theberge, M.T. (2004) *The Wolves of Algonquin Park: A 12 Year Ecological Study*, ISBN 0-921083-67-X, 180 pages.

236

55 Andrey, J. and Knapper, C., editors (2003) *Weather and Transportation in Canada*, ISBN 0-921083-65-3, 305 pages.

54 Bunch, M.J. (2001) *An Adaptive Ecosystem Approach to Rehabilitation and Management of the Cooum River Environmental System in Chennai, India*, ISBN 0-921083-62-9, 484 pages.

52 Nelson, J.G., Butler, R. and Wall, G., editors (1999) *Tourism and Sustainable Development: Monitoring, Planning, Managing, Decision Making*, ISBN 0-921083-60-2, 406 pages.

51 Olive, C. (1998) *Land Use Change and Sustainable Development in Segara Anakan, Java, Indonesia: Interactions Among Society, Environment and Development*, ISBN 0-921083-59-9, 350 pages.

50 Needham, R., editor (1998) *Coping with the World Around Us: Changing Approaches to Land Use, Resources and Environment*, ISBN 0-921083-58-0, 294 pages.

48 Mitchell, C. and Dahms, F., editors (1997) *Challenge and Opportunity: Managing Change in Canadian Towns and Villages*, ISBN 0-921083-56-4, 298 pages.

46 Sanderson, M. (1996) *Weather and Climate in Kitchener-Waterloo, Ontario*, ISBN 0-921083-54-8, 122 pages.

45 Andrey, J., editor (1995) *Transport Planning and Policy Issues: Geographical Perspectives*, ISBN 0-921083-53-X, 261 pages.

43 McLellan, A.G. (1995) *The Consultant Geographer: Private Practice and Geography*, ISBN 0-921083-51-3, 230 pages.

40 Sanderson, M., editor (1993) *The Impact of Climate Change on Water in the Grand River Basin, Ontario*, ISBN 0-921083-48-3, 248 pages.

39 Lerner, S., editor (1993) *Environmental Stewardship: Studies in Active Earthkeeping*, ISBN 0-921083-46-7, 472 pages.

38 LeDrew, E., Hegyi, F. and Strome, M., editors (1995) *The Canadian Remote Sensing Contribution to Understanding Global Change*, ISBN 0-921083-45-9, 462 pages.

37 Nelson, J.G., Butler, R. and Wall, G., editors (1993) *Tourism and Sustainable Development: Monitoring, Planning, Managing*, ISBN 0-921083-44-0, 306 pages.

36 Day, J.C. and Quinn, F. (1992) *Water Diversion and Export: Learning From Canadian Experience*, ISBN 0-921083-42-4, 236 pages.

35 Mitchell, B. and Shrubsole, D. (1992) *Ontario Conservation Authorities: Myth and Reality*, ISBN 0-921083-41-6, 388 pages.

34 Mitchell, B., editor (1991) *Ontario: Geographical Perspectives on Economy and Environment*, ISBN 0-921083-37-8, 311 pages.

30 Coppack, P.M., Russwurm, L.H. and Bryant, C.R., editors (1988) *The Urban Field, Essays on Canadian Urban Process and Form III*, ISBN 0-921083-25-4, 249 pages.

29 Guelke, L. and Preston, R.E., editors (1987) *Abstract Thoughts: Concrete Solutions: Essays in Honour of Peter Nash*, ISBN 0-921083-26-2, 332 pages.

27 Nelson, J.G. and Knight, K.D., editors (1987) *Research, Resources and the Environment in Third World Development*, ISBN 0-921083-23-8, 220 pages.

25 Guelke, L., editor (1986) *Waterloo Lectures in Geography, Vol. 2, Geography and Humanistic Knowledge*, ISBN 0-921083-21-1, 101 pages.

24 Bastedo, J.D. (1986) *An ABC Resource Survey Method for Environmentally Significant Areas with Special Reference to Biotic Surveys in Canada's North*, ISBN 0-921083-20-3, 135 pages.

20 Mitchell, B. and Gardner, J.S., editors (1983) *River Basin Management: Canadian Experiences*, ISBN 0-921083-16-5, 443 pages.

19 Gardner, J.S., Smith, D.J. and Desloges, J.R. (1983) *The Dynamic Geomorphology of the Mt. Rae Area: High Mountain Region in Southwestern Alberta*, ISBN 0-921083-15-7, 237 pages.

Occasional Papers

20   Cukier, J., editor (2006) *Tourism Research: Policy, Planning and Prospects*, ISBN 0-921083-74-2, 320 pages.

19   Wall, G., editor (2003) *Tourism, People, Places and Products*, ISBN 0-92-1083-66-1, 272 pages.

18   Scott, D., Mills, B., Jones, B., Svenson, S., Lemieux, C., Wall, G. and McBoyle, G. (2002) *The Vulnerability of Winter Recreation to Climate Change in Ontario's Lakelands Tourism Region*, ISBN 0-92-1083- 64-5, 100 pages.

17   Wall, G., editor (2001) *Contemporary Perspectives on Tourism*, ISBN 0-921083-63-7, 304 pages.

16   Wall, G., editor (1993) *Impacts of Climate Change on Resource Management of the North*, ISBN 0-921083-47-5, 270 pages.

15   Wall, G., editor (1992) *Symposium on the Implications of Climate Change for Pacific Northwest Forest Management*, ISBN 0-921083-43-2, 244 pages.

13   Sanderson, M., editor (1991) *Water Pipelines and Diversions in the Great Lakes Basin*, ISBN 0-921083-39-4, 131 pages.

12   Wall, G., editor (1991) *Symposium on the Impacts of Climatic Change and Variability on the Great Plains*, ISBN 0-921083-38-6, 376 pages.